Right Relationship in the Real World

Learning to Live by our Unitarian Values

Commissioning Editor:

Jane Blackall

The Lindsey Press
London

the unitarians

Published by The Lindsey Press
on behalf of The General Assembly of
Unitarian and Free Christian Churches
Essex Hall, 1–6 Essex Street, London WC2R 3HY, UK

www.unitarian.org.uk

ISBN 978-0-85319-099-8

Designed and typeset by Garth Stewart

Contents

Preface

Hucklow Summer School, a week-long gathering of Unitarians for religious education and personal development, has taken place annually since 1995. Typically, 50–60 people take part in this intensive residential week, held at the Nightingale Centre in Great Hucklow, Derbyshire; however, during the Covid-19 pandemic, a series of online talks was offered in place of the in-person event.

In setting the agenda for Summer School each year, we try to discern a theme that is live and timely for us: what is it that we are wrestling with in this moment – as a movement, as a society, as a species? What might we currently be neglecting, or overlooking, as a community, that needs attention? How might we live out our faith more wholeheartedly and put our Unitarian values into practice? We are conscious that our choice of theme might shape the conversation in the wider movement. Those who participate in Summer School are often changed by the experience. When they return home, this influence radiates outwards, as a little (or a lot) of what they have gained is passed on to others, through sermons, newsletters, and conversations.

In 2022, when, for the third consecutive year, the theme talks could be offered online only, our theme was *'Right Relationship: Practising Love, Peace, and Justice in Everyday Life'*. Over the course of the week our team of speakers explored the idea of 'right relationship': with self, with others, and with God. Each night, a different pair of speakers (working collaboratively, to reflect the relational theme) took on the topic from a different angle. The brief was to reflect on what living in 'right relationship' might require of each of us in our closest connections with friends and family ... in our congregations and wider communities (local and online) ... with people near and far with whom we rarely come into direct contact, and whose life experiences are very different from our own, but with whom our existence is interdependent ... and with the Earth itself.

For Summer School in 2023, held in person for the first time since 2019, our chosen theme was *'Real Life: Telling the Truth of our Lived Experience'*. We experimented with a different format for our theme talks, presenting a series of shorter reflections for discussion, all given by a single speaker. We also went hybrid for the first time, offering those who could not attend in person a chance to participate remotely. During the week we explored what it means for us to truly 'be real' – with ourselves, in our relationships, in our communities, with God – and how we can make space for others to do likewise. The talks focused on sharing the truth of what life is really like for us, and being curious and compassionate about what life is really like for others, especially those whose lives are invisible to us and whose voices are unheard. We also reflected on how the distinction between 'real' and 'virtual' has been blurred over the past few years, as the new communities and relationships that we have created and sustained online have shown themselves to be equally vital and valuable, particularly for those who were excluded or isolated by their personal circumstances from many 'real world' opportunities for connection, engagement, and participation in community life.

I am delighted that, thanks to The Lindsey Press, these thoughtful talks will reach more people in print form, and I am hopeful that the questions for reflection included at the end of each chapter will encourage congregations to set up small groups to explore the themes more deeply and keep the conversation going.

Jane Blackall
Convenor of the Hucklow Summer School Panel

PART ONE

Right Relationship: Practising Love, Peace, and Justice in Everyday Life

(Summer School 2022)

1 What Do We Mean by 'Right Relationship'?

Sarah Tinker and Jane Blackall

PART ONE – Sarah

Surely the Summer School Panel have come up with the ultimate topic this year: *Right Relationship*. It's all in there, isn't it? Life, the universe, the whole caboodle – expressed in that pleasingly brief concept.

We have searched for the origins of this terminology, and (although we can't be sure) it seems to have appeared first in writings connected with the Society of Friends. Not surprisingly, as Quakers have long encouraged one another to reflect on their relatedness to other human beings, as well as to God. We have them to thank for the ever-useful injunction *'Recognise something of God in everyone you meet'*, which some of us use as a guiding principle to this day. In Unitarian circles I have heard that re-stated as *'Recognise the spark of divinity in all that exists'* – thus widening the context beyond the merely human. And later in this talk I will consider the Sufi guidance expressed in the words *'This too is me'*.

The term 'right relationship' reminds us of the Noble Eight-Fold Path of Buddhism, also known as the Three-Fold Way, where three aspects of Buddhist life – ethics, meditation, and wisdom – are expanded. Established way back in the 5th century BCE, some of these edicts sound so modern. Maybe they can guide us in life now.

- Right action (behaving in a skilful way and not harming others)
- Right speech (speaking truthfully)
- Right livelihood (earning a living in a way that does not harm others or cause suffering)
- Right mindfulness (being aware of yourself and the emotions of others)

- Right effort (putting effort into meditation and positive thoughts and feelings)
- Right concentration (developing focus so that you are able to meditate)
- Right view / understanding (remembering that actions have consequences)
- Right intention (being clear about following the Buddhist path)

Again, I will come back later to this idea of guidelines for our relating. But the fact that we have such clear guidelines from ancient times is a sign that the issue of how we get along with one another has been around as long as members of our species have been living together, and no doubt it applies to our earlier kindred too. Clearly we are relational creatures, we depend upon one another, and we have been establishing rules and guidelines about how to live with one another since our earliest days of communicating.

Is anything different in the 21st century? Maybe not, although in some societies the unfettered rule of power and force is challenged in ways that would not have been possible in centuries past. We could argue that the remarkable development of social media as a means of relating digitally has brought us many new issues to consider, as well as many new possibilities for ways of relating. And in Western societies such as Britain we have seen a notable shift in attitudes towards authority, a growing awareness, and sometimes distrust, of hierarchical relationships.

So here we are in 2022, a little gathering of Unitarians, asking ourselves how might we establish right relationships? How might we best practise love, peace, and justice in everyday life? In this session Jane and I are particularly focusing on relatedness with ourselves and with others. And I may as well break the bad news to you sooner rather than later – although this probably dawned on all of you a lot sooner than it dawned on me – that there is no static, happy-ever-after, whoop-de-doo, 'in-right-relationship' state to arrive at, after which we can all relax. Like balancing on a bicycle, in our relatedness we will be for ever in motion; re-adjustments both subtle and large will for ever be required of us. And although on this first evening we are exploring the personal elements of right relationship, we also need to establish that every element of human existence is inter-connected. Ethics, the legal system, economics, politics, world affairs, the natural world, and environmental crises – all play their part.

As does history. We cannot forget that for much of human history people throughout the world have been treated differently because of gender, because of race, because of age, because of social class and economic status – to mention but a few of the myriad ways in which we humans differentiate ourselves. To take just one example, it was only in the 19th century in English law that the long path towards women being regarded as equals with men began. Children were regarded then as a father's property. Married women had no rights over their own property. But dissenting voices became louder, campaigns were fought, and eventually they led to changes in the law. Slowly, greater gender equality was established, and women gained the right to vote. You know the story. But we still have a gender pay gap in the twenty-first century: women in the UK are paid 90 pence for every £1 paid to a man. Ten per cent less. And the statistics on violence against women should horrify us all. It can be painful to realise how much further we need to work towards equality. And to recognise that humanity's steps forwards can so quickly slide backwards once more when there is regime change.

Legal systems and economics are crucial aspects of relatedness, yet in this area of personal relationships that we are considering in this session are we not hoping that each individual will take some responsibility for right relationship – because rules and legislation can only go so far? It's worth mentioning here the work of Martin Buber, a prominent twentieth-century philosopher, religious thinker, political activist, and educator. His most famous work explored two ways of human relating to our world, which he named as *I–Thou* and *I–It*. Both forms of relating are needed in human existence, explained Buber in his philosophical essay *I and Thou* (1923). In *I–It* relationships we relate to people and objects through their function. Only in *I–Thou* relationships is true dialogue possible, true sharing, with no masks or pretence. But Buber was clear that such connections were inevitably fleeting, that we move in and out of *I–Thou* relatedness, that it can never be constant or static.

And I would add that such depth of relating is potentially both wonderful and exasperating. It's certainly not easy to interact authentically, is it? Particularly in on-going relationships. Is this not where love needs to be invited in, again and again and again? Earlier this evening I smiled when Jane read 'To Invoke Love', a poem by Revd Sean Parker Dennison, which includes a description of love not arriving in the form that perhaps we had hoped for.

> *To invoke Love*
> *is to never know if it will come softly,*
> *with the nuzzle of a beloved dog,*
> *or pounce right on your chest with the strength of a lioness*
> *protecting her cub, her pride, her homeland.*[1]

In the realm of personal relationships, you have probably noticed, things rarely go quite according to plan.

PART TWO – Jane

What do we even mean by 'right' relationship? As that is the theme of the whole week, I think we had better put that gnarly question on the table on Day One. To speak of 'right' relationship implies that there is such a thing as 'wrong' relationship (and, you have to imagine, a great big grey area in between, which is the space where most of us live, most of the time). People, especially liberal-leaning people, can sometimes be a bit allergic to the very notion of 'right and wrong', a bit averse to any hint of moral absolutes, a bit inclined to moral relativism. And of course that's the territory we are in: when we talk of 'right relationship', we are talking about morality and ethics, asking perennial questions such as 'How should we live?' or, in any given moment or situation, 'What

---

1   Sean Parker Dennison, *Breaking and Blessing: Meditations* (Skinner House Books, Boston, 2020).

should I do?'. The very presence of the word 'should' in those questions implies the existence of a moral or ethical norm that we are holding ourselves to – that there is a right answer to such questions (and a wrong one) – or perhaps that there is a whole spectrum of answers that could somehow be graded according to their degree of rightness or wrongness.

Ethics and moral reasoning is an enormous topic, and it is not my intention here to get bogged down in the academic aspect of things (although I have done a bit of study in that field). The scholarly side of ethics which speaks of utility, duty, and virtue is fascinating to explore and reflect on, but it can be hard for us to join the dots between such theoretical moral calculations and the way we choose to act each day – how we live our lives in messy reality. Even if, in principle, we lean towards one of these theoretical approaches to ethics, working out what it means for our conduct – the 'right' thing to do in any given moment – is by no means straightforward. Our lives are interwoven in such a complex web of interdependence, each move we make (or fail to make) in any moment can set in motion a chain of events with infinite reach and unknowable consequences (think of the Butterfly Effect); you would have to have a God's-eye view of the entire Universe to be able to truly weigh up the impact of every action before you make it.

As an aside: this puts me in mind of a splendid routine from the comedian Bill Bailey. He talks about a typical exchange of greetings between British people:

'How are you?'
'Not too bad, all things considered.'

Whenever anyone says *'not too bad, all things considered'*, Bill Bailey says he wants to reply: *'What, you've considered ALL things? The tectonic plates inching around the planet, mocking our brief dance on the surface? Everything that has ever existed at a molecular level? The uncountable stars? The boundless universe beyond which our imagination founders on a distant shore?'*. (That's a highly abridged version of five minutes of escalating absurdity featuring marmite, manatees, Franz Liszt, and the tears of a Patagonian shepherd ... and I clearly can't do justice to Bill Bailey, so do look for it on YouTube for the full joyful experience.) My point is: we can't really consider ALL things when it comes to making ethical decisions in everyday life.

So if this moment-to-moment moral calculus is a bit of a non-starter, how do we *really* make our ethical decisions in everyday life? How do we judge what 'right relationship' means in practice? I am mindful of the words of the moral philosopher James Griffin in his book *Value Judgement: Improving Our Ethical Beliefs:*[2]

> We inherit our ethical standards. We start our moral life with firm
> views about right and wrong, some so firm that they are never
> shaken. Still, in time we start rejecting others of them. We do
> not just change our minds about them; we also find them faulty
> in some way – unjustified, out of date, too undiscriminating. We
> regard our new ethical beliefs as not just different, but better. Much
> moral philosophy should be seen as a continuation – more self-
> conscious and more sustained – of this project of improvement that
> all of us are engaged in before we have even heard of philosophy ....
> Our ethical standards are hand-me-downs, and sooner or later we
> start criticising them. How should we go about it?

So, as James Griffin says, none of us work out our ethical standards from first principles: we absorb them from our family, our culture, our peers. Some we cling to unquestioningly; some we examine and retain; some we reconsider and reform; some we outgrow and reject altogether. Plenty of what is passed on *will* stand the test of time. But – I hope – as individuals, as a community, as a society, we do have it in us to reflect and grow. Many people here tonight have seen huge shifts in society in their lifetime; for example, homosexuality was illegal not so long ago – anti-gay sentiment was absolutely the default moral position in our society; but now, on the whole, the consensus has moved on – thank God – to the point where same-sex marriage is a thing, and on the whole

---

2   Oxford University Press, Oxford, 1998.

people can be safely 'out' in most spheres of life (although I need to acknowledge that there is a significant backlash against this progress around the world right now).

Nevertheless, we should expect our moral principles to evolve and change as we integrate new insights gleaned from our collective experience. I find myself thinking of the well-known quote from Maya Angelou: *'I did then what I knew how to do. Now that I know better, I do better.'* I would venture that, perhaps, the longer we have held on to a certain moral precept, the more ingrained it will be in our sense of self, and the harder it will be for us to revise it. What does it say about the person we were before? We might feel a sense of shame about our previous outlook, and that can be a very powerful force, resisting necessary change. There is a great deal of moral courage involved in coming to the conclusion that some long-held moral principle of ours was misguided, mistaken, or just plain 'wrong', and changing our view (and our conduct) accordingly. And in addition to those internal dynamics we can find ourselves almost trapped in a certain moral world-view by tradition, peer pressure, social norms, and misguided notions of 'common sense'. Just because it's 'normal' doesn't mean that it's 'right'. That is one of my key messages in this theme talk. I can hear a thousand mothers saying *'Just because everyone else is doing it doesn't mean that you should'.*

Many ways of being with each other in our society today are, in my view, a million miles away from 'right relationship'; but harmful conduct often goes unquestioned (or is even celebrated), just because we are used to it, and *'it's the way things are and the way they have always been'.* Every day of our lives we will see cruelty, exploitation, bullying, neglect, and carelessness all around us (to varying degrees) – if we are paying attention. There is bad behaviour in workplaces and schools (and, yes, churches); in the media, where it is often excused, minimised, or passed off as entertainment; on social media, which have a reputation for being a cesspit, and where *'I was only joking! Can't you take a joke?'* is used to excuse all manner of nastiness. In so many settings, harmful conduct is all too often accepted, normalised, perpetuated, even reinforced by institutional structures and social norms. But so often we prefer not to speak of it, not to name out loud what we have witnessed, not to cause a fuss, not to be the awkward sod who initiates the difficult conversation about harm; and really this is understandable, as speaking may well result in negative consequences. There have been some laudable high-profile campaigns recently where behaviour that was widely considered socially acceptable in the past has been challenged, and perpetrators have been 'called out' for the harm that they have done. I am thinking particularly of the 'Me Too' campaign, initiated by the American activist Tarana Burke, which raised awareness of the prevalence of sexual harassment and assault – particularly in workplaces: it was (and is) going on *everywhere*. And everybody *knew* – it was almost a clichéd joke in every TV sitcom of my childhood – but it's only now that the tide seems to be turning, and it is taken seriously as being 'wrong', rather than just laughed off and dismissed as something that only bra-burning feminists were bothered about.

All of which is to say: the first step towards cultivating right relationship is to question everything! Don't just assume that the 'right' thing to do, or the 'right' way to be, is obvious, or 'common sense', or that it's what everybody else is doing. Don't just default to going-with-the-flow in order to fit in socially. I realise this is a bit paradoxical (going out on a limb socially does make it harder to be in relationship at all!). But if we are framing this in terms of attempting to live 'right', discerning how to act more ethically, then we are talking about reflecting on our way of being in the world, rather than living on autopilot. And – as James Griffin has warned – this will quite likely involve deconstructing and discarding some of the habits of thought and action that we have inherited, and going our own way. And we can't stop there! It's not enough to reject what has gone before. Having *de*constructed, we need to *re*construct. If we have discerned that some or all of what we inherited is 'wrong', then the next step is to work out what we are going to put in its place, rather than leaving a moral vacuum. What *are* our moral commitments? And what values, principles, or foundations are they based on?

One of the key purposes of church life, as I understand it, is to be a community which reflects on ethical questions such as these – a community which affirms values, principles, and moral teachings – a community in which we hold each other accountable in striving to 'know better and do better'. Of course, a church is more than an ethical society. But it is one important aspect of what we do.

In communities such as ours, it can sometimes seem that we lack enough shared reference points to come to a consensus about what is 'right' and 'wrong'. We Unitarians frequently speak about the importance of each person searching their own conscience. In Cliff Reed's classic text, *Unitarian? What's That?*,[3] I found no fewer than ten mentions of conscience in that slim volume. Just a few excerpts:

> We hold that all people have the right to believe what their own life experience tells them is true; what the prompting of their own conscience tells them is right. ...
>
> On all issues of personal conscience, each Unitarian is free to come to his or her own conclusions without fear of judgement or censure. ...
>
> A Unitarian view of sin might be: to sin is wilfully to act, speak, or even think in a way that one's own conscience condemns as wrong. ...
>
> To be a Unitarian is to take responsibility for one's own faith. It is to value the intuitions of oneself and others. It is to test one's beliefs against reason and conscience. It is to afford others the same right to be honest with their own inner authority as one claims for oneself.

Conscience is actually a big deal for Unitarians. But conscience can be a bit of a slippery concept, and – am I being too cynical here? – occasionally I wonder if people use the appeal to conscience as a shorthand for *'I'll do what I like, thank you'* (just using it as a form of self-justification without actually doing the deep reflection needed to back it up).

....

3   Cliff Reed, *Unitarian? What's That? Questions and Answers About a Liberal Religious Alternative* (London, The Lindsey Press, 2018).

When I was studying with the Jesuits at Heythrop College a few years back, I was introduced to a way of thinking about conscience that has shaped my understanding of the concept ever since. Briefly – as I understand it – the idea is that we don't just get born with an 'oven-ready' conscience. Conscience must be *formed* and *informed*. Formed and informed. Conscience is, crucially, formed *in community*: we draw on many sources of moral wisdom, over time, to *form* our conscience: that is, to develop our capacity for accurate perception, reflection, and analysis of moral matters. (This goes back to what we have already considered: sifting through our moral inheritance and the cultural norms that we have acquired to see what is worth keeping and what we should chuck away.) And then, in any given situation, conscience requires us to be properly *informed*: to find out all the relevant facts (and to discard what is irrelevant, distorted, or untrue), so that our conscience has got good data to work with when discerning the 'right' course of action. To live by conscience is demanding.

But to nurture our conscience is to cultivate a place within ourselves where the voice of God may be heard. And that is how I conceive of this notion of 'right relationship': it's about aligning our way of being in the world with some 'North Star' which guides us towards love, truth, and beauty. It's about reflecting on our way of relating to self and other – including other creatures, the natural environment, our planet, the entire universe beyond it – and reaching towards the Greater Good. For me, that 'North Star' is something that I am happy to name 'God', but you might name it differently.

Still, however we conceive of it, we need to discern what is required of us in each moment – what God requires of us, what Love requires of us, what Justice requires of us – in order to live in 'right relationship' (or something a bit more like it) with self, other, and God, in our everyday lives. Even our best attempts at sincere discernment will rarely result in conclusions that we can be 100 per cent certain and confident about (and often we will have to make a leap and act before we are really sure).

So perhaps we should just aim, as best we can, to do 'the next right thing', perhaps bearing in mind the wise saying from Ignatian spirituality: each of us can only discern 'for me, for now, for good'.

PART THREE – Sarah

Some of us humans put a lot of effort into discerning how we should best behave in relationship with others. Just take a look at those shelves filled with self-improvement titles in bookshops or online. And I suspect quite a few of us will have come away from time spent with others and chewed anxiously over what we, or they, said or did, or how we could have handled things better. Not surprising then that human groups and societies create laws, rules, and guidelines to try and help us establish right relationship.

I mentioned the Buddhist Eight-Fold Path earlier on. We have Moses staggering down the hillside with the Ten Commandments. We have Jesus' graceful response when asked which was the greatest of those Commandments:

> Jesus replied: "'Love the Lord your God with all your heart and with all your soul and with all your mind'. This is the first and greatest commandment. And the second is like it: 'Love your neighbour as yourself'. All the Law and the Prophets hang on these two commandments."[4]

Various cultures and religions have developed versions of what became known as The Golden Rule: do unto others as you would have them do unto you. As a Religious Education teacher years ago, I led some happy lessons in which students explored the many versions of this rule and designed a poster illustrating all the ways in which we could treat people nicely. But there was usually at least one thoughtful teenager who would query whether everyone on this planet would actually want to be treated as we want to be treated. Aren't we all different? And of course we are. The so-called Platinum Rule (platinum being considerably more valuable than gold) has been variously attributed and suggests that we should treat others as they would wish to be treated. It is certainly an improvement,

---

4   The Gospel of Matthew, chapter 22.

because it elicits an empathic response to the other person. It requires us to be interested in them, rather than leaping to assumptions about how they would like to be treated, basing our conclusions on our own preferences. We need to discover, through dialogue, what the other person wants and needs. But that presents problems too. Some people would want to be treated in ways that are not in their own best interests or the interests of the wider grouping. People's yearnings have to be balanced against the wants and needs of others.

So laws about relationships can be very helpful indeed in protecting us. Rules and guidelines can be useful ways of clarifying required behaviours in particular settings. But all such codes have limitations and drawbacks. And when we enter the area of personal relationships, we are stepping into a space where there is little clarity about the 'rules'. It is open for negotiation. No wonder we get into a mess! I have long had pinned on my noticeboard this little statement:

> *I know that you believe you understand what you think I said,*
> *but I'm not sure you realise that what you heard is not what I meant.*

It makes me smile in rueful recognition of just how very tricky communication in our relationships is – so tricky that I can't imagine ever claiming that I was in right relationship with anybody. I think the best I would ever say is that I and others are fumbling around trying to communicate effectively with each other, trying our best to understand each other, doing what we can to express what is inside us, how we are thinking and feeling, what our hopes and dreams currently are, alongside our fears and anxieties. Working on our communication skills has to be the key way in which to build right relationship. And what might that look like? Probably different for each of us – but for me I have to overcome blocks of niceness, anxieties about upsetting someone, fear of the other and what I might hear. I have to carve out time to actually be with the other person, because communication takes time, far longer than I am often ready to give to it. Building right relationship requires me to lean in towards another person, rather than backing away when there is a difficult situation. Are not most of us quick to back off when things get difficult or heated, or awkward and embarrassing? Fill in your word here for the personal situations that you dislike the most. Fellow Unitarian Michaela Von Britzke urges the need for 'sturdy intimacy' in our church relationships, as a way to overcome the shallow, superficial niceness of our culture.

And along with that sturdy intimacy, we have to develop our skills of curiosity, of gentle questioning, of expressing our interest in another person. We have to be willing to express our confusion and to seek clarification. We have to rein back our assumptions and any illusions that we can read another person's mind. When we develop such skills, we help the other person to self-disclose. We encourage them to tell us something of themselves, to express their vulnerability. This ability to tell others something intimate about ourselves is one of the first planks of the bridge that we hope to build between ourselves and another. It says: *I'm here, I'm vulnerable like you, I'm interested in you, tell me more.*

And let us not forget that when it comes to personal relationships we do need to be alert to the differences between us in terms of power and privilege. That is not said in any way to put us off seeking relatedness with people who are different from us. Because that is exactly what our world needs: more of us getting to know people who are different from us. But when some of us already have a more established place in the world, when life is stacked in our favour, then it is our job to stay aware.

To invoke Love
is to give up self-deprecation, false humility, pride,
to consider yourself worthy to be made whole,
willing to encounter Love that will never
let us let each other go.[5]

---

5   Sean Parker Dennison, 'To Invoke Love', in *Breaking and Blessing: Meditations* (Skinner House Books, Boston, 2020).

PART FOUR – Jane

My first encounter with the phrase 'right relationship' was, if I remember rightly, just over twenty years ago. I came across the concept when Thandeka, the Unitarian Universalist minister and theologian, visited our General Assembly meetings to give the Essex Hall lecture in 2002. In this lecture, Thandeka introduced the notion of Engagement Groups to Unitarians in the UK, as a very particular way of gathering people together in small groups within our congregations. These groups are also known as 'Covenant Groups' or 'Small Group Ministry' – I think there are a number of variations on the theme – and, when they are run properly, they are transformational. Indeed, our Summer Schools, when we are able to gather in person at the Nightingale Centre in Great Hucklow, are built around these Engagement Groups. So I am positively evangelical about this sort of small-group process.

But – take note – not every small group is an Engagement Group. You can't just stick a dozen people in a room (whether in-person or on Zoom) and call it an Engagement Group. Nope. The defining characteristic of an Engagement Group is its particular *purpose and intention*. The way the groups are formed, and framed, and facilitated is all determined with that purpose in mind. And – for twenty years now – I have been repeating this purpose over and over to myself and anyone else who will listen: the *defining purpose* of Engagement Groups is to bring people into right relationship with themselves, each other, and God (or that which is of ultimate worth).

I know some people here tonight will be very familiar with participating in Engagement Groups, or leading them, and I expect there will be others for whom the concept is new. My own understanding of the purpose and intention of these groups was influenced by *The Covenant Group Source Book*, published back in 2000 by the Center for Community Values in Chicago (which was founded by Thandeka). It defines them as small groups of up twelve people who meet on a regular basis to cultivate beloved community; the intentionality and regularity with which they meet helps to build strong relationships between participants, and also strengthens connection and commitment to the wider congregation of which they are a part. These groups vary in their focus: members might gather to share their life stories, read scripture or poetry together, do craft projects, work together on social-justice issues to serve the community – but whatever the particular activity with which the group is engaged, it will ultimately be a space for growth, caring, and connection. Engagement groups are structured in ways which embody our Unitarian commitment to affirming the inherent worth and dignity of every person, and our place in the interdependent web of life. As the Covenant Group Source Book states: '*Together, people establish communities which embody the values of justice, democracy and human dignity. Each person is treated equitably. Each has a voice and is heard. And each person is respected for his or her own intrinsic humanity. The defining purpose of [an Engagement Group] is to bring people into right relationship.*'

Why am I telling you about this? Well, partly, I admit, in the hope that some of you will be at least a little curious about the big claims that I am making for the transformational power of these groups for individuals, and communities, and the wider world. Maybe a few of you will be as intrigued and inspired as I was by the prospect, you will read up about how to do it, and you will take the leap, as I did, to set up an Engagement Group of your own, in your congregation, or another setting. But mainly the point that I want to make tonight is that you can think of Engagement Groups as a case study in *cultivating the conditions for right relationship.* And by considering some of the typical features of an Engagement Group, we can learn some lessons for life-in-general.

Quite often when people participate in an Engagement Group for the first time – or at least, this was the case 15–20 years ago, when the idea was first gaining traction in our denomination – they can find it a bit awkward. Uncomfortable. Because, *by design*, Engagement Groups interrupt our usual habits of conversation in order to enable something *better*. Engagement Groups are *counter-cultural*; they help us intentionally to unlearn some of the harmful habits of behaviour that are prevalent in the wider culture, which undermine 'right relationship'. These groups generally have their own covenant, a set of agreed ground rules, tailored *to* the group *by* the group. At Summer School we usually offer groups a set of suggested 'ground rules' (along with the rationale behind each of them), and a facilitator encourages people to stick to them once they have been agreed.

So in these groups we encourage people to share their stories, their truths, their authentic selves, and to listen to each other without comment or interruption – without turning it into a head-y debate, or butting in with our own brilliant anecdotes – and when what we hear in these groups is difficult or complicated, we refrain from trying to 'fix' anything or 'make things better'. What we are called to be is loving witnesses to each other. In the words of Parker J. Palmer (Quaker educator, activist, and founder of the Center for Courage and Renewal): 'When you speak to me about your deepest questions, you do not want to be fixed or saved: you want to be seen and heard, to have your truth acknowledged and honoured.'[6]

In my experience, in groups with these sorts of ground rules, covenants act as a sort of 'scaffolding' – or perhaps more like a set of 'training wheels' – a source of stability and support to hold us upright while we get the hang of this way of being with each other that is ... different. They create a safer space where we can take a few more risks, be a bit more vulnerable, go deeper. Perhaps be more real with each other than we might typically manage at coffee hour on Sunday. And, crucially, they are spaces where everybody gets an equal chance to be heard; those voices that usually dominate are required to make space for the voices that are usually dominated. In the 'Heart and Soul' contemplative gatherings that I run – on Engagement-Group principles – I always say *'This is a space where silence is welcome, and we don't rush to fill it'*. In other words, *'We're doing something different here – don't worry about keeping up the chat'*. And when we create such spaces, we may discover that other voices – the ones that are usually crowded out – find the courage to speak into the space that has been created.

One other feature of Engagement Groups that supports right relationship is that they are based on autonomy and consent. So many of the everyday situations in which we find ourselves involve some degree

---

6   *A Hidden Wholeness: The Journey Toward an Undivided Life* (Jossey-Bass, 2009, p. 117).

– whether overt or subtle – of compulsion or coercion. Perhaps it's not something that you are especially aware of in your own life – it is perhaps more obvious to those who are less privileged, or less powerful, in various ways: those whose choices seem more limited, those who feel they can't afford to say 'no' or 'rock the boat' by going against the flow in social situations where others have more power and status. But I would imagine that most of us can think of occasions when peer pressure has bounced us into doing something that we didn't want to do. Engagement Groups, at their best, start from a point of really respecting people's autonomy, and operating on the basis of genuine consent. The group facilitator might present a suggested covenant or set of ground rules to the group, but it is an invitation for each person to accept, or reject, or negotiate, until they are happy to proceed on these 'terms of engagement'. The facilitator explains what activities are planned, so everyone knows what's coming up, and each can make an informed decision about whether or not they are willing to be part of it. While everyone is encouraged to join in, it is typically made explicit that this is an invitation, not an obligation – there is always a 'pass option' – and sitting an activity out, or finding an alternative way to participate, is a genuine option; participants know they are not going to be socially punished for opting out. Because one of the foundations of right relationship is *consent*. I think there is perhaps a widespread lack of awareness of consent issues in everyday life, and I wish I had more time to unpack this – and to give you some examples of 'doing consent better' in daily life, and congregational life – but I wanted to flag it as something that deserves more attention.

The point of telling you about Engagement Groups is this: some of the most valuable ways of cultivating 'right relationship' are quite hard to sustain unilaterally in a world where our culture and our economic system train us to treat people like *things* – valuing others only in so far as they are 'useful' or 'productive' – rather than treating each person as an infinitely precious soul with the inherent worth and dignity that we so often speak of. When we intentionally and repeatedly practise deep listening, authentic sharing, making space, and honouring consent in Engagement Groups – all of which are practices of right relationship, practices of love in action – we begin to internalise ways of being which spill out into the rest of our lives, our congregations, and eventually the wider world. We truly encounter other people, we hear their stories, and we begin to understand and appreciate the infinite variety of human identity and experience just a little bit better.

We listen. We learn. And we love.

PART FIVE – Sarah

This term 'right relationship' inevitably asks us to question where we are getting things wrong. A quick scan of the world's news will spotlight some of the areas that I reckon most of us would agree are in need of healing: our relationship with our home, planet Earth, our race relations, gender inequalities, attitudes towards migrants, issues of identity, our treatment of animals, to mention but a few – and some of these will be explored by other speakers later this week.

But in this section this evening, as we consider our relationships with ourselves and our personal relationships with others, I want to encourage our processes of self-examination in life. I am not going to use the famous quotation attributed to Socrates that 'an unexamined life is a life not worth living' – because I imagine that you, like me, have met people who live simply and lovingly, and don't spend hours worrying about what so-and-so said, or about the choice that they made yesterday. There are many ways to be human, and an unexamined life can be a life filled with love and beauty. Those of us who are blessed, or cursed, with busy minds and turbulent emotions – we are the ones who need to hone our reflective powers. We are the ones who need to be aware of the gaps in our awareness and to seek actively any opportunities that might assist us in understanding other people better.

As a Unitarian minister I want to trumpet the possibility of using our churches, our congregations, as places of exploration and education. Churches are a great resource, and they are one of the places where we might occasionally meet people who are different from us. I wonder if there are people whom you are particularly glad to have met in a church setting. For me it was gay men. I don't know why, but 30 years ago I had never knowingly met a gay man, to speak with and listen to in depth, until I began attending Unitarian events. That changed my life. It gave me new perspectives on the world. It taught me a painful and useful lesson about my oh-so-human tendency to generalise about groups of people. I am embarrassed to remember the gently humorous way in which I was put right about some of my assumptions. And of course, before too long, spending time with members of a minority shattered any illusions that I had had about our Unitarian movement and its supposed openness to all. I heard stories, true stories, of ignorance and oppression: someone losing their post as a minister because of their support for equal marriage, gay couples ignored at social events, congregations that quietly let it be known that their pulpit would never welcome someone who was 'openly' in a gay relationship. This was nigh on thirty years ago. I sincerely hope that such attitudes have changed. But there will always be new issues for us to be educated in. We are late as a denomination to be considering our inherent racism, and the work of awareness raising is unfairly left to just a few people. We are at the start of an educational process on trans issues. We are as dangerously slow as many other parts of our society to respond appropriately to the climate emergency.

Minority groups rightly tell us that it is not their job to educate us. Can we utilise our church resources to take on this educational work? Indeed, is that not what this Summer School week is all about? Education. Sharing our insights. Telling our stories. Bringing one another some new perspectives to consider. Making space for other voices. Only by such processes of personal and collective education, processes of consciousness raising, can we develop ourselves as potentially useful allies for invisible and oppressed groups.

The digital realm enables us to hear some of those other voices that most of us would not encounter in our everyday lives. We can now read and hear about other people's experiences and their needs. And perhaps that can then strengthen us in seeking out face-to-face encounters with those who are not like us in various ways. It can be salutary to realise what bubbles many of us live in, confining ourselves to groups and situations and individuals that mirror ourselves. I believe that taking a step towards the 'other', rather than away from them, is a vital task for our world society now. It may well be a tentative, hesitant step. It may well lead us to realise how little we can actually offer the 'other'. But it is a step of great spiritual significance to face one whom we do not know, do not understand, may even fear, and genuinely hold that Sufi message within our very being: *'This too is me'*. We are one. And all this, dear friends, is easier said than done.

> *To invoke Love*
> *is to guard against assumptions,*
> *take care with our words and practice forgiveness,*
> *not as ethereal ideal, but right here,*
> *in the messy midst of our imperfect lives.*[7]

PART SIX – Jane

To live in right relationship – with ourselves, with others, with our planet and all its inhabitants, with God (or whatever we consider to be of ultimate worth) – that is a beautiful thing to aspire to. And, as we have just begun to explore this evening, it is potentially quite a demanding aspiration too.

I don't know about you, but I am finding life quite tough these days, in a variety of ways. The last few years have been particularly hard-going for many of us: so much loss, change, and uncertainty – so much conflict and instability on both a local and a global scale. It's relentless, and it wears us down. And I wanted to acknowledge that fact, as we bring this talk to a close, because when we are struggling and feeling besieged as individuals, we might find it quite a bit harder to extend ourselves to others. We might find ourselves instinctively drawing inwards for self-preservation. Like a little armadillo.

---

7   Sean Parker Dennison, 'To Invoke Love', in *Breaking and Blessing: Meditations* (Skinner House Books, Boston, 2020).

So, as we begin to draw this first theme talk to a close, I want to remind you of the need for balance. On the one hand, yes, let's strive to know better and do better, to change ourselves and the world. Let's do that rigorous self-examination that Sarah was talking about, and let's not be complacent. Let's do what we can to resist and disrupt the ways of the world that inhibit right relationship.

BUT: let's remember to be in right relationship with ourselves too. Because we need a bit of self-compassion in the midst of all this. There is a balance to be struck between, on the one hand, this wonderful, virtuous, noble striving for change and, on the other hand, the need for acceptance of the limits of what *we* can personally do (especially given that the world is burning, the Covid virus has not gone away, and many of us are variously dealing with hardship, insecurity, and trauma on a daily basis as the world seemingly unravels). It is understandable that we might not always manage to put our best foot forward in the circumstances. It would be understandable if we just stayed in bed and refused to come out from under the duvet. And yet we aspire to something more.

Despite our best efforts, we are bound to screw things up on a fairly regular basis, in relationships of all kinds. We are likely to say or do the 'wrong' thing (or fail to say or do the 'right' thing) – to disappoint and hurt each other. Perfection is unattainable, and it's good to keep that in mind right from the start. So this is a reminder to lay off the self-flagellation when things go awry! Life is tough enough already. Most of us know people – and it might be you – who tend towards self-sacrifice and martyrdom, who instinctively give themselves away for the sake of others, and risk burning themselves out altogether in the process. AND: most of us know people – it might be you – who tend to lean the other way, towards self-interest, and away from engaging with other people's needs. Perhaps more often it's not so much due to active selfishness as to a passive *lack of interest* in others. Still, I suggest that we each need to discern and maintain some kind of proper balance between compassion for self and compassion for others. The two are inextricably linked in any case; I cannot help but recall these wise words of Parker J. Palmer: 'Self-care is never a selfish act – it is simply good stewardship of the only gift I have, the gift I was put on earth to offer others. Anytime we can listen to our true self and give it the care it requires, we do it not only for ourselves, but for the many others whose lives we touch.' [8]

Over the next four evenings we will hear a number of perspectives on 'right relationship' in context. I am looking forward to the insight, the inspiration, and – no doubt – the challenges that we've got coming to us! So, in the days to come, let's bear in mind that balancing act. Let's keep our aspirations high – even if we know that the messy realities of life mean that we will probably fall short – and let us be kind to ourselves when we do. We try, we fail, and we will try again, in our attempts to practise love, justice, and peace in our everyday lives, as we try to help create a better world. Still, let us set our sights on that vision of right relationship – with self, other, and God – and may it be so, for the greater good of all.

Questions for reflection and discussion

1. What is your understanding of the role that conscience plays in 'right relationship'?

2. When have you seen the 'Platinum Rule' in action ('Treat others as they wish to be treated')?

3. Can you recall a time when your world-view shifted after listening to someone whose life experience was very different from your own?

---

8   *Let Your Life Speak: Listening for the Voice of Vocation* (Jossey-Bass, 1999, pp. 30–31).

The authors

Revd Sarah Tinker attended the first-ever RE Summer School in Great Hucklow in 1995, at the start of her involvement with our Unitarian & Free Christian movement – and it changed the course of her life. Moving from her job as a secondary-school teacher to work as RE & Youth Officer for the General Assembly, she eventually underwent ministry training and served for 15 years as the Minister with Kensington Unitarians at Essex Church. Having now stepped back from congregational ministry, she remains involved with many aspects of Unitarianism. She sees our Unitarian chapels as resources for the whole community, providing spaces for people to meet and engage in the work of building right relationship. And she believes that our congregations are communities where we can work together to create a kinder, fairer, and more sustainable world.

Revd Dr Jane Blackall has been a regular attender and speaker at Summer School since the year 2000 and has been closely involved in organising the event since 2005. She worked in the field of medical imaging and radiological sciences, gaining her PhD at Guy's Hospital, King's College London, before studying Philosophy, Religion and Ethics at Heythrop College and training for the Unitarian ministry. She is now the Minister with Kensington Unitarians, based in central London at Essex Church, but reaching out since 2020 to include a widespread community of Unitarians around the country and worldwide via online ministry. Jane is increasingly energised by the potential of online spiritual gatherings to include those who find it hard to participate in traditional in-person services because of factors such as disability, ill health, neurodivergence, geographical isolation, work commitments, or caring responsibilities. In recent years she has co-developed and co-facilitated LGBTQIA+ training on the theme of 'Working on Our Welcome', to increase awareness and sensitivity on issues of gender, sexuality, and relationship diversity, and to help make our congregations more hospitable.

2 For Those Who Are Not In The Room

Nicola Temple[1]

Chalice words

We light this chalice for the people who are not in the room.

May our circle of light fall upon those on the margins; the vulnerable and forgotten, those trapped at home by illness and age, those who feel judged, excluded, ashamed, in pain.

May our warmth hold those with precarious lives; carers and struggling parents, those juggling work, life, and bills, the exhausted and burnt out, anyone who is just trying to get through the day.

May our flame inspire those who share our principles and feel they carry the grief of the world alone. May they find us, and may we be stronger together.

May we go out and walk beside those who are not in the room, whoever they may be. May we do this sacred work with open arms. May we break down the walls and hold all in our expansive and loving embrace.

(by Lizzie Kingston-Harrison)

---

1   Lizzie Kingston-Harrison and Nicola Temple collaborated on the original theme talk on which this chapter is based. Nicola would like to thank Lizzie for her wonderful friendship, support, and encouragement throughout the whole process, and without which the publishing of this chapter would not be possible.

Introduction: who isn't in the room?

In this talk I wish to explore what it means to be in 'right relationship' with others by inviting you to explore what it means to have a spiritually healthy relationship with the people who are not in the room. In the broadest sense, this includes people who are unable to attend our services and other congregational activities, those who are unable to access what we have to offer for all sorts of emotional and practical reasons, and even those who do not want or need to be with us. This theme is inherently and gloriously paradoxical, it is a blessing to explore it, it is challenging, illuminating, and expansively loving.

I hypothesise that it is good spiritual practice, wherever you happen to be and whatever you happen to be doing, to ask yourself 'Who isn't here?'. Draw comparisons with who is in the room. Explore why that may be. This is about cultivating an attitude of love and curiosity: a great antidote to the fear of the unknown and the other. As Jane has said to us, we have an ethical responsibility to question the status quo, and we do not need to accept what we see, or assume that it is the only way to be.

I would love it if you left our talk tonight driven to ask that question – 'Who isn't here and why?' – about your own chapel or meeting house, and feeling empowered to do so in conversation with others in your congregation.

Some of the people who are not yet in the room need to be with us; we have gifts to share with them, and we have a place at our table for them. Just as importantly, we need them too! Their gifts, and their love and joy and creativity, their brokenness, and challenges. We need them. We need to be curious and ask 'How can we meet the needs of the absent folk, and how might they enrich our lives?'. Of course, for our congregations to survive we need more people in the room, but this talk is not about church growth. It is about how we establish a healthy relationship with ourselves, with God, with each other, and how that foundation will inevitably open up new spaces for new people to engage with us.

* * * * * *

The US Lutheran pastor Nadia Bolz Webber in her blazing book, *Cranky Beautiful Faith*,[2] describes her attempt to come into the Unitarian room. I wanted to be a Unitarian 'so badly', she writes. 'Unitarians are such smart, good people. They vote Democrat and recycle, and love women and they let you believe anything you want to.' But she couldn't pull it off, because she needed a specific, external source of divine love and reconciliation – grace – that she eventually found elsewhere. Fair enough. Clearly some people are not in the room because the theology doesn't sit right. And part of being in right relationship with them is to acknowledge that we cannot serve everyone, and that we will not be the right fit for everyone. The grace we can offer is not the washing away of our flaws, vulnerabilities, mistakes, failings, and shame, but the acceptance of them, the acceptance of ourselves and each other as fully human, and the healing that comes from that. This talk is based around this idea: that at the heart of a good relationship is the empathic act of hearing, seeing, and meeting someone on their own terms, and that this dynamic act invites love in and is both a unifying moment and an opportunity for change.

Building relationships

Alongside the invitation to ask, and keep on asking, the question 'Who is not in the room?', I have three suggestions that may help you establish a right relationship with the people who are not in the room.

1. I suggest that it is an act of grace to congruently and lovingly relate to someone as they are, without imposing our judgements or our own needs. This is the heart of the right relationship, and creating a space where this habitually happens will draw new people in and keep them there. They will know that this is a space of healing. The mindfulness teacher, Tara Brach, calls this 'radical acceptance', and

---

2   *Cranky Beautiful Faith: For Irregular (and Regular) People* (Canterbury Press, Norwich, 2013).

it begins with the people in the room and then radiates outwards. Brene Brown, in her work on shame and vulnerability, says the same. She suggests that re-engaging people with institutions like churches means first establishing spiritually healthy relationships with each other, as a way of opening up spaces that people actually want to come into. If we build our rooms like this, they become places for everyone.

2. I suggest that not everyone should be met in the room as it exists right now. While there are some people whom we need to invite in, to sit at our table, there are other people who need us to redefine the room. They need us to meet them where they are, and to walk alongside them.

3. I suggest that both the above conclusions necessitate growth and change and new ways of reaching people, and that this is healthy for us all. *But* I also wish to emphasise that that is not the same as compromising our principles or losing our unique voice in order to conform to wider culture. In fact, the opposite is likely to be true. In a context where neo-liberal values, materialism, capitalism, and disregard for the planet are commonplace, there has never been a better time to come alive to our principles, to share them and live them in new ways.

Down through generations ...

In recognition of the contradictory and rather amorphous nature of the theme, this talk is grounded in personal experience and reflection. In being honest and authentic about my own story I hope to sit in right relationship with all of you too. Because this is mostly personal, I have not tried to speak for other people. This is not a list or an overview of all the types of people who may not be in your congregations, and what you can do about it – because only you can do that work. It is a personal reflection on the barriers that face some people who are 'a bit like me', and I have focused my reflection on generational differences.

According to the 36th British Social Attitudes survey, conducted by the National Centre for Social Research in 2018,[3] religious affiliation (of any kind) has a 'half-life' of one generation. While we may bristle at the comparison of faith with radioactive waste, it is a neat way to describe the significant decline in religious belief in the UK. Secularisation in Britain is generational, and trends indicate that this decline has been happening for approximately the last 200 years. Individuals are not giving up their religion. It is simply that secularisation is generational. We lose those with religious belief – and they are replaced with those who have none.

Of the people surveyed in 2018, 52 per cent said that they had no religious affiliation; 66 per cent never attended any kind of religious service, apart from social occasions such as weddings and funerals; 21 per cent said they had no confidence in churches or any religious institution.

I am unusual for my generation. Only 36 per cent of 18–34-year-olds have a religious affiliation, 29 per cent attend religious services of any kind, and 33 per cent believe in God. In the 35–54 age group, the proportions are only slightly higher than in the younger generation: 43 per cent have a religion, 32 per cent attend religious services, 40 per cent believe in God. While optimists suggest that there is evidence of people 'believing but not belonging', or that spiritual practices such as yoga or meditation are filling the gap, there is little evidence to suggest this in the data.

---

3   British Social Attitudes 36 | National Centre for Social Research (natcen.ac.uk)

My story: having religion and being Gen Z

Who am I?

Here are some elements of my own story, how I became involved with the Unitarians, and what I perceive to be some of the barriers to faith engagement that people face.

My story begins in Chester, where I was born in 1997. I am 25 years old and am in the upper end of the Generation Z age bracket. I was brought-up in a stereotypically average middle-class family, and I was lucky that exploration of the world around me was strongly encouraged, and that I was supported by my parents throughout my childhood and teenage years. I was raised in the Church of England, and my parents are still very actively involved in the city-centre Anglican parish church that we attended as a young family. As with many churches, across different denominations, the congregation at this church in the early years of this century was ageing, with most regular attenders above retirement age and only a couple of families with children under 18. As a result, I have never found it unusual to be the youngest person in the room – often by some decades.

My introduction to Unitarianism came through my grandmother, who has been a member of Bayshill Chapel in Cheltenham for much of my lifetime. When I was 15, Granny took me along to Summer School for the first time, and well – here I am today! My teenage experiences of Unitarianism, through attending occasional services with my granny and making return trips to Summer School, made a lasting impression. Although I was (and still am) actively involved with the Church of England, and maintain a Christo-centric personal theology, Unitarianism taught me to question and challenge established ideas, and to broaden my outlook beyond the cosy middle-class existence of my childhood.

Upon finishing school at the age of 18, I attained a place at the University of Liverpool, to study Avionic Systems Engineering. As is the case for many young people leaving home, university offered me new levels of freedom and the opportunity to gain new insights and experiences. I loved living in Liverpool, making new friends, exercising my new-found independence, and occasionally even doing some studying; but what I personally valued most was the opportunity to strike out on my own faith journey and step away from what, to my teenage self, felt like a tired, out-of-touch and sometimes stifling Anglican tradition. I became a member of Ullet Road Unitarian Church in Liverpool and engaged in as many Unitarian activities and opportunities as I could find.

As with all wonderful things (and I admit that I am possibly guilty of viewing the past through rose-tinted spectacles), my halcyon days at university came to end and, three years ago, I moved away from Liverpool and the congregation at Ullet Road church. I now live in rural Bedfordshire, I have a job as an RF (Radio Frequency) Systems Engineer, and I am very actively involved in my local Anglican church.

Why am I in the room?

I hope that brief summary of my background explains a bit about how I came to be involved with Summer School and the Unitarians, and how I have landed where I am today.

I don't currently regularly attend a local Unitarian congregation. One reason for this is that there simply are no congregations that are less than an hour's travel away. I go to my local village Anglican church most Sundays; I engage with local parish activities, and meanwhile I maintain a 'long-distance' involvement with the Unitarians when I can. This has included being an Associate Member of the General Assembly; subscribing to *The Inquirer*; undertaking voluntary roles with Summer School and the GA Youth Programme; and remote membership of #Blessed, which is a young-adult group mainly based in Gellionnen Chapel in South Wales.

As you might have gathered, my faith is important to me, and it is deeply personal! In her own theme talk, Jane mentioned the concept of establishing a right relationship with 'God (or that which is of ultimate worth)', and for me a relationship with God underpins my faith and my continued church attendance. I have grown up in an environment where religious observance and spiritual practices are a regular part of my weekly routine. Attending church or chapel services gives me time and space in my week to pray, reflect, take stock, and leave worries and anxieties with God. It gives me spiritual nourishment and a breathing space away from the incredibly busy and sometimes chaotic rhythms of day-to-day life.

For me, spiritual practices are tools that I use to help me navigate my way through life; and church communities should provide a safe, supportive space in which to practise one's beliefs. But another reason why I like to engage in a church or chapel community is for the social aspect. I have many varied and deep friendships that have come through church connections. Through church life I have met people of many different backgrounds, ages, and nationalities. This makes for deep, rich relationships and broadens my own outlook and understanding of the world.

Chapel communities can also provide a strong and natural platform for social-action projects. This is something that I have particularly experienced through my participation in #Blessed. As a chapel youth group, #Blessed focuses on local community-action projects that are normally small enough to be achievable, ambitious enough to give a sense of purpose, and worthwhile enough to have a noticeable impact on the local community. It is hugely rewarding to feel able to make a difference and give something back.

Why are people (particularly my generation) not in the room?

After listing all the reasons why church membership works for me, the question arises – why are there not more people attending chapels or churches, or generally engaging with religious congregations?

I am sometimes asked 'As a young person, what do you think we need to do to get more young people involved?' The irony of asking one person who already attends about the general mindset of the large group that doesn't attend sometimes seems to get lost. The honest answer is that I'm already here, and I don't really know and couldn't presume to speak on behalf of the people outside the door. But there are a few questions to consider when looking at lack of attendance in particular age groups:

1. Is this a behaviour correlated to age, or are there other societal factors at play, and is this trend seen across all cultures, or just across communities in the UK?
2. Where it is age-related, is this a behaviour that is going to continue throughout the lifespan of the generation in question, or will people 'age out of' or 'age into' certain beliefs as they get older?
3. How far are we currently seeing just the most recent section of a long-term trend that has been developing over the past several generations?

In the time available for this talk, I cannot offer detailed analyses of these questions, but there are clearly complex multi-faceted factors at play. These include societal developments, geopolitical changes, and scientific advancements which mean that religion does not feature much in many people's lives. It is also possible that some of this generational divergence has led to myths, stereotypes, and preconceptions putting people off exploring religion and church communities. For example, there might be a perception that churches are necessarily homophobic, or anti-science. Unfortunately, it seems that the generational decline is here to stay, and it is difficult to see a magic quick-fix solution to change this.

I have established what I perceive to be the problem and I have admitted that there is not going to be an easy solution, so perhaps it is time to stop shaping this as a problem and instead view it as an opportunity. We know that people are not engaging with religious communities, and we can hazard guesses as to why: children not being brought up to go to church; religion being viewed as irrelevant in a world in which science explains everything; perhaps, as in my case, simply an absence of local congregations; or even just a feeling that 'it's not cool'!

So, the real questions that we first need to ask concern the people that do engage in church communities:

- how do they engage?
- why do they engage?
- and what do they look for if they are looking to join a new congregation?

By offering spaces for the people who do already come, and leaving our doors open to welcome the newcomers and the tentative seekers, we are already making a small step in the right direction.

What motivates people to get involved?

Firstly, it is important to acknowledge that every individual who comes through our doors has their own reason for entering, their own life experience, and their own skills and capabilities. Any balanced relationship involves an ebb and flow of giving and taking. Everyone who comes into our communities has things that they seek to gain, and things that they wish to give. Examples of things that people may be seeking from a chapel community include:

- spiritual connection and possibly a relationship with God or a Divine being
- community connection and a social or support network
- knowledge or understanding, by which I largely mean possible answers to some of the big moral, social, and/or spiritual questions that we face.

At the same time, people will often feel more satisfaction and fulfilment if they perceive that they 'add value' and can give something back into a community. This might be material or financial, or probably more commonly an offering of time and skills that can be seen to make a difference.

The next thing to remember is that everyone has their own limits and expectations. It is important in any relationship to recognise the balance between giving and taking, and also to realise that a healthy balance will lie in a different place for each of us.

I would like you to join me in imaging a purely hypothetical chapel community:

- It is difficult to say how big this community is, but it contains a wide demographic of members and often gets visitors coming in to join services and other chapel activities.

- The chapel holds one Sunday service each week, regularly hosts community events and social evenings, and actively engages in local social-action projects.
- One member of the congregation attends approximately one service a month. They consider this to be a huge achievement, as they have to work their attendance around two jobs and looking after a sick family member, but they value their time at the services for the respite and spiritual engagement that they find there.
- There is another member of the chapel who is always there at every service. They find spiritual fulfilment in the services, and their life centres around the chapel activities that involve the regular congregation. They are seen as a pillar of the chapel congregation, but they might be quite shy to engage in wider community initiatives.
- A third member of the chapel community has a sporadic attendance at the Sunday services, but will always turn up to support any wider community events and is keen to facilitate wider community engagement.

The question I would now ask is 'Do we consider each of these people to be equally valid members of our chapel community?'

There are some people for whom chapel begins and ends with a Sunday service. And there are some for whom what matters more than the services are community interactions. I would suggest that either of these approaches, and all the ones in between, are equally valid. Each member of our community brings what they are able (and want) to contribute, and they should be able to find the nourishment that meets their individual needs. As such, chapel participation can come in various forms and guises. Congregational development should focus first on the needs of the people who are present in their different forms, and then use this as a foundation from which to look further afield into the wider community.

If we want to explore our relationships with the people who are just outside the room, we perhaps need to define where the walls of the room are, and think about whether we can push the walls of our room out to include the people with whom we maybe, at the moment, have only a tangential connection.

Are there people who can't access the room?
This talk has mainly focused on some of the motivations that drive different people's engagement with religion. In addition, however, there are some practical issues that should always be considered when we assess the walls of our room:

- Do we have appropriate means of access in place to enable everyone to feel valued and to be able to attend with dignity?
- Do we make our services accessible for those with neurodiverse needs?
- Are our services and events always scheduled for the same time each week? Can people in work or with family commitments be there at the times in question?
- Do we have space for children within our chapels and worship spaces? Are there tensions between child-care issues and chapel attendance?
- Do we take monetary collections in a way that might exclude or embarrass people who struggle with low incomes or stretched finances?

These issues are very real and can be the make-or-break question for some people when it comes to being able to attend services or engage with Unitarian activities. Please do consider all those who want to be in the room, or who might otherwise tentatively step into the room if it weren't for all the arbitrary physical, financial, and logistical barriers that we put up in their way.

Being in right relationship

Sometimes bringing people into the room is about creating spiritually healthy relationships with ourselves, the divine, and each other, and then drawing others close in our embrace. When we truly hold someone, we open our arms and invite them into our space to show that we include and accept them. The 'platinum rule' is a variation of the more familiar golden rule and can be simply described as treating others as they would like to be treated. Holding people in right relationship means putting the 'platinum rule' into action; recognising the unity of right relationship in a spiritual sense; and realising that we are not separate, and we all have a place at the table.

Sometimes relating to the people not in the room will mean inviting them into our space. At other times it will look like going out, taking down the walls, and creating new spaces and new ways of doing things so that we can meet people where they are. If people are not in the room, then we need to expand the room.

I am grateful that I can be in this room with all of you. Thank you to everyone here who has found a way to work online, to use social media, and to start groups that work around jobs and families and responsibilities. Thank you to everyone who has had to let go of things that no longer work, and to those who have reimagined our Unitarian traditions and rituals in a way that has made them relevant to us, the younger generations. I am here because Unitarians from older generations have met me, invited me in, walked with me, and encouraged me. I am blessed to be in the room, and I urge that we must all now be part of the sacred work of creating space for others to join us.

Questions for Reflection and Discussion

1. Who is and isn't in the room at your chapel or meeting house?

2. Why are you part of your congregation? How does it nourish you, and what do you bring?

3. How have you defined your 'room'? Is there a way in which you can 'expand your walls', and remove barriers to participation, by expanding your sense of what counts as 'church'?

4. What can you do to try and ensure that your congregation is a place where right relationships are prioritised? Do you agree that this will help to bring new people 'into the room'?

The author

Nicola Temple has been involved with the Unitarians since she first attended Hucklow Summer School as a teenager. She grew up in the north-west of England and for some years was a member of Ullet Road Church in Liverpool. She now lives in rural Bedfordshire, where she enjoys walking and connecting with the outdoors. Nicola is deeply curious about the world around her; in her free time, she loves to read, swim, and solve cryptic crossword puzzles, while in her professional life she works as an Avionic Systems Design Engineer. Nicola is currently unable to attend a Unitarian congregation locally, so she attends her local Anglican Church.

3 Building Right Relationship with Our Embodied Selves

Arek Malecki and Laura Dobson

PART ONE – Arek

This talk continues the theme of right relationship. Here we will consider building right relationship with our embodied selves. It is a deeply spiritual subject, so we would like to suggest that you take some time to centre yourself before you delve further into the topic. Before you turn the page to read on, simply settle into a brief time of prayer, meditation, reflection – whatever you call this act of 'praying attention'. And when you're ready, turn the page to read the words of a specially written prayer.

Prayer

There is no prayer.
This is not a prayer.
No, seriously – sorry to have fooled you.
Sorry to have interrupted this moment of bliss
You might have anticipated.
To compensate you for that, we will provide you
With some meditative tools at the end of this chapter.

There is no prayer.
Our apologies for playing this trick on you.
But we must ask: what did you do to prepare yourself
For this time of not-a-prayer?

Did you adjust your body?
Did you sit more comfortably?
Did you move to your favourite spot in the house?
Did you drop your shoulders?
Did you steady your breath?
Did you adopt any kind of prayer pose?

* * * * * *

We didn't tell you what to do, we did not encourage you to adjust yourself. But we are willing to bet that, if you accepted our invitation to join us across the dimensions of space and time in a moment of prayer, you made at least some adjustments to the way you sat. And if not, next time you find yourself in a religious gathering, either in-person or online, simply pay attention to what people around you do immediately before a time of prayer. Is this an innate instinct, or a learned behaviour? A conscious choice or a subconscious habit? Sometimes it can be mildly entertaining to observe how we have Pavlov'ed ourselves to make such adjustments automatically when we hear the phrase 'Let us pray', or a variant of it.

For now we leave you to ponder on the question of why you 'adjusted yourself', as we ask you once again to settle in and return to your breath. This time – no dirty tricks. We promise. No unnecessary interruptions. Simply:

Breathe with me
Breathe with me—the breath of life
Inhale, Inspire, Inspiration,
Ruaḥ, Pneuma, Spiritus, *the Holy Spirit*
the many names for breath.

Breathe with me.
Know that with each breath we take in molecules of air
that were breathed by every person that ever lived.

Breathe with me,
and breathe the breath of Jesus, of Moses,
of Mohammed, of the Buddha.

Breathe with me,
and know that we are all interdependent,
that the spirit of life flows through us all.

Breathe with me,
as we come together to do the holy work
of interconnection and relationship,
that our work here may be blessed.[1]

What is embodied spirituality? What does it mean to have the right relationship with our flesh? How can this possibly translate into right relationships with our communities, and ultimately with all existence?

---

1   Matt Alspaugh, https://www.uua.org/worship/words/prayer/breathe-me. Used with permission.

We wonder whether our Unitarian denomination occasionally downplays the fact that we *are* bodies in our approach to spirituality. Not always, of course. But by and large our spiritual engagement is predominantly intellectual. To put it bluntly: Unitarians love talking. We love words and intellectual engagement. And this is all good – as long as we make room for our bodies too. We enjoy mind-**FULL**-ness (using this term very loosely here): having our minds filled up to the brim. But, as the philosopher Alan Watts once famously said, 'A person who thinks all the time has nothing to think about except thoughts. So they lose touch with reality and live in a world of illusions. By thought I mean specifically: chatter in the skull – perpetual and compulsive repetition of words, of reckoning and calculating.'[2] Can we learn to appreciate bodyfulness as much as we appreciate mind- FULL-ness?

Have you ever heard people saying that 'we are not human beings having spiritual experiences: we are spiritual beings having human experiences'? This phrase often crops up in pop-spiritualities of today. Although we appreciate the rhetorical goals of people who use this expression, we feel the need to challenge it, because it seems to negate the incarnational aspect of our being. It downplays how incredibly important to our experience of spirituality is the fact that we have bodies. Nay – we do not just 'have' bodies. We *are* bodies. Feminist theologian Elisabeth Moltmann-Wendel wrote that 'having a body' is our predominant experience. You have a body for working, running, carrying, loving, eating, dancing, doing the things you love to do, and the things you have to do. Our experience is that the body functions. That is, it does what we want it to do … until, despite our best efforts, it doesn't! We become insecure, we may lose the rhythm and framework of our everyday life. It often takes such a crisis for us to have another experience. Namely, that we *ARE* bodies. We realise that a body is not just a thing attached to our head. It is not something that we have. It is us.

Grossly oversimplifying history, it may be fair to say that the church distrusted the body for centuries on end. This was partly rooted in certain

---

2   https://www.youtube.com/watch?v=zBCxCU_omZ4

interpretations of the Christian scriptures. In the New Testament Greek there are two distinct words referring to a body. *Soma* typically refers to 'body' in a greater sense – the body of the church, the body of Christ. *Sarx*, on the other hand, means 'flesh' – the impure, repugnant bag of meat, bones, and all sorts of bodily fluids. This flesh has needs, some of which needed to be repressed. *Sarx* is an instrument, a tool. And it is potentially very dangerous. You may not be surprised to learn that in the world-view that proposed such a dichotomy a man was often perceived as representing the head, the intellect, and the spiritual dimension of being human; while a woman, or rather female body, was precisely this: *body*. Flesh that needed to be kept in check. There were, of course, throughout church history, numerous people who challenged such an artificial division. Many of them were women. We want to tell you a little about a few of such influential women of faith, as well as about the experience of *being a body*, told from the perspective of a woman today.

PART TWO – Laura

I would like to start by sharing some of my experience of adapting and re-framing my spiritual practice over the last few months as I navigate the changes in my body brought about by perimenopause. It took me quite a long time to recognise what was happening to me. Menopause is not something that we discuss in 'polite society', and as such it was a mystery to me until I enlisted the help of the internet, and eventually my doctor.

The fact that it was a mystery to me is part of what seems to be a modern aversion in Western society to acknowledging ageing and the workings of our bodies, particularly women's bodies. But we are our bodies. Our bodies carry our ancestral identities and our personal stories. Unless we are skilled in astral projection, all of our earthly experiences happen in and through our bodies. I have always been keen on spiritual practices that are grounded in physicality.

Students training for the Unitarian ministry are encouraged to explore what spiritual practices they find nourishing, and to develop a regular practice routine. I developed a morning practice which usually included a body prayer, a short yoga routine, some singing or chanting, and maybe some free-form dancing if I was feeling particularly energetic that day. These are all practices that help to ground me in my body and set me up for the day. But as my symptoms increased, I noticed myself developing a strong resistance to my morning spiritual practice. I won't bore you with the whole raft of perimenopausal symptoms, but suffice to say that they include brain fog, increased anxiety, persistent fatigue, and intermittent joint pain, which are all things that can make me feel dislocated from my body.

On reflection, I felt that part of my resistance to my spiritual practice routines was a reluctance to attend to what is happening in my body, to be with the discomfort there, and sometimes the pain. I wasn't sure what to do about it. I have never been much good at sitting still, and I knew that spiritual practices that did not involve movement would not really work for me, but most mornings I was finding it hard to motivate myself to move very much. I realised that I needed to re-frame my spiritual practice and adapt it for this phase of my life. Engaging with the work of three inspirational women and one inspirational man has helped me to do that.

The first inspirational woman is Hildegard von Bingen, who lived from 1098 to 1179 in the Rhine Valley in Germany. She was a Benedictine abbess and a polymath: she composed what was perhaps the first opera ever written, and approximately 75 liturgical songs; she also wrote nine books, covering theology, holistic medicine, cosmology, ethics, scriptural commentaries, and biographies of saints. She completed several preaching tours and wrote more than 300 letters to leading political and religious figures, in which she often challenged hypocrisy and corruption. Neglected by the church for centuries, Hildegard's work has re-emerged only relatively recently; the first collection of her writings, translated into English, was published in 1983: *Meditations with Hildegard* by Gabriele Uhlein. She was made 'Doctor of the Church' by Pope Benedict XVI in 2012, one of only four women to hold that title.

There are two concepts found throughout Hildegard's work that I find helpful in considering the idea of well-being: in Latin these are named *viriditas* and *discretio*. Viriditas can be roughly translated as 'greening'. Hildegard used it to mean the life-force, vigour, or vitality of both plants and people. She used it to refer to what we now understand as photosynthesis, the power of plants to harness the energy of the sun; and she also used it to refer to human sexual desire. In terms of well-being, viriditas can be thought of as what allows us to flourish and thrive. Discretio is sometimes translated as 'moderation', but it has a greater depth of meaning. It also means discretion, discrimination, discernment, difference, and distinction.

When we put these two concepts together in the context of right relationship, we can use discernment as a guide in relation to our life-force. Hildegard's view of life included the belief that God created balance in the body, and order in the cosmos. Discretio is the practice of *living* that balance, or order, in the union of human and divine, finding harmony of body, mind, and soul. It involves paying attention to our inner compass, the promptings of our bodies and our deep selves, to find the right measure in all things.

We can use discretio to find the right measure for ourselves in all aspects of life: the balance between work and leisure, between activity or exercise and rest, and between sleep and wakefulness. We can use discretio to work through such questions as: What does a balanced diet look like for us? How do we find the right measure for ourselves in our consumption of communications media? How do we live with awareness of our natural environment and seasonal changes? Are our relationships reciprocal? Is there a balance between the care that we give out and what we receive?

Discretio involves taking responsibility for our actions and choices. We can use it to examine our habits, social conditioning, and unconscious thought-patterns, and make the changes that we need to flourish and thrive. Balance involves an on-going process of interconnection. The physical, emotional, intellectual, and spiritual dimensions of our lives are interwoven. When balance is disturbed, we experience disease – dis-ease. Even a minor illness such as the common cold affects all these dimensions. We may think of it as a physical illness, but as well as making us feel physically ill, it affects our emotional mood, how well we function intellectually, and our sense of interconnection and wholeness. The psychological and physical symptoms of menopause are similarly interwoven. Anxiety, brain fog, and mood swings exacerbate palpitations, tingling skin, and headaches, and vice versa. It can feel like being trapped in a vicious circle. Here is what Hildegard says about discretio:

> Discretio is the mother of all virtues for everything heavenly and earthly ... always looking for the justice of God in all things ... God gives us the virtues as tools to accomplish his work. Live by the Golden Mean. Don't build a ruin through exaggeration, or ruin yourself with excessive desire. We shall sigh and pray, fulfilling good deeds at an appropriate time and caring for our daily needs at another. Try hard and exercise daily – regardless of what charismatic gifts you have ... through discretio the body is nourished with the proper discipline.[3]

I began to ask myself what Hildegard might teach me about my experience. What are the lessons of viriditas (greening) and discretio (discernment)? What is stopping me flourishing? How can I discern the truth of the matter? How can I be more at ease with myself and my situation? How can I find the right measure? These are on-going questions that I keep coming back to again and again. Just like life itself, perimenopause is not an entirely linear journey. The right measure might be different for me on different days. Some days I need lots of rest to replenish my viriditas. Some days I can replenish it with gentle exercise, such as a leisurely walk in the woods, or 15 minutes of yin yoga. Some days it might be some chanting and breath-work that helps me to feel in tune with the flow of life.

---

3   Matthew Fox (ed.), *Hildegard of Bingen's Book of Divine Works* (Bear & Company, Rochester, Vermont, 2001).

PART THREE – Arek

Right from the start of ministry training, students are encouraged by their tutors and mentors to find a spiritual practice that works for them. And if you happen to study for your theology qualification at the Luther King Centre in Manchester, you are likely to be asked to develop your own Rule of Life. The Rule of Life is a set of 73 regulations compiled by Saint Benedict of Nursia, governing life at his monasteries. It is not an exaggeration to say that I was terrified when I was told that I would have to write my own Rule of Life, Benedictine style, and try to abide by it. (To make matters worse, it was done as a part of an academic assignment, so it seemed that I had little choice.) I couldn't remember signing up to be a monk when I signed my learning contract. The very word 'rule' was so off-putting to me. David Runcorn, in his *Spirituality Workbook*,[4] wrote that we react in this way because the very term 'sounds impersonal and authoritarian, and that human and spiritual progress is surely not for measuring against a precise straight edge of a rule'. This particularly rang true for me as a Unitarian. After all, I don't call myself a freethinker and nonconformist for nothing! But the Latin for rule – *regula* – seems much gentler. It suggests a signpost or a handrail. It appears to be more nurturing, a tool that can offer support or direction in your journey of life and of faith. It is something to lean on.

As suspicious as I was about formulating any rules, I had to realise that my life had lately become chaotic. Suddenly many of the unwritten rules governing my days (which I detested so much) had vanished. The year was 2020. Firstly, there were all the Covid restrictions which turned upside down my (thus far) predictable life. Secondly, after ten years of climbing the corporate ladder, I resigned from full-time employment to train for church ministry. My structured life was taken over by disorder. I was not able to distinguish my rest times from my work or study times. Time for household chores blurred with time for entertainment.

----

4   David Runcorn, *Spirituality Workbook: A Guide for Explorers, Pilgrims and Seekers* (SPCK, London, 2006).

Everything seemed to merge into one and became formless. To make it worse, everything in my life took place in the same space, in front of the same screen, due to pandemic lockdowns. I began to wonder whether, perhaps, I did actually need at least some of those previously despised patterns in order to function. I discovered that this total lack of structure and composure was a curse.

As someone who suffocates in a world of regulations, who dislikes rigid structures, rarely plans, and allows life to simply carry him where it will, I knew that I had to frame my rule in rather vague terms too. If my Rule of Life was too detailed, I would fail from the very first moment. I knew that trying to write 73 chapters of my own Rule would defeat the object, as Benedictine emphasis on stability is not some piece of abstract idealism: it is typically realistic. Words like 'stability' and 'balance' get repeated in all literature that deals with the Benedictine rule. I wondered, however, whether this stability should be the end in itself, or whether it is simply a means to reach a different goal.

I am suspicious of approaching life as a whole with a certain end in mind, be it a vision of career, life achievement, or even heaven, nirvana, or whatever after we die. I concluded that instead of beginning with an end in mind – which would suggest that I might eventually arrive at that destination – I ought to begin with a point in mind. It struck me that the days of St Benedict's monks were constructed on the rhythmic succession of three elements: prayer, study, work. Four hours each day were devoted to liturgical prayer, four hours to spiritual reading, and six hours to manual work.

Although Chapter 48 of the Rules states that 'idleness is the enemy of the soul', the structure of the monks' days was not conditioned by their productivity. Rather, it was about the time spent on each task. This was a significant discovery for me. I needed to unlearn the idea, perpetuated by the capitalist system in which we live, that my worth is measured against my productivity. St Benedict did not say how many acres of land his monks were supposed to plough, or how many chapters of the Bible they must read before they were allowed to move on to the next part of the day. Instead, their days were divided into segments of time. This was the lightbulb moment for me. As a person who self-diagnoses with severe time-blindness, I struggle with regulating the time that I spend on individual tasks. As soon as something catches my interest, my hyperfocus kicks in and I become completely consumed by it.

As I began to work on my personal Rule of Life, I needed to consider what really is the point (not the end goal!) of life for me. This highly existential question cannot possibly be explored here. Many books have been written about it, and many great minds have wrestled with it. However, since many people suggest that the Rule of Life is simply a tool to help us become more human, then the life that it is seeking to govern must also be a life that is unapologetically human. A life that takes the incarnational aspect of our being seriously. I began to wonder: what things make me feel alive in the moment, connected to the divine, to the Universe?

Stability, balance, as the Rule describes it, is fundamental. It is something much more profound than not running away from oneself. It means acceptance of the totality of each human as a whole person, involving mind, spirit, and *body*.

I am scatter-brained and I found it difficult to identify something in which I could comfortably anchor my spiritual practice and not get easily bored with it. For months, if not years, I have been trying to practise stillness, meditation on words, and spiritual reading of scripture or poetry. Those sometimes worked. To a limited extent. Annoyingly, I was often left frustrated when the words fell flat – that was when my ears heard what was being said, but my brain refused to register the meaning of it. Worshipping in a group, I often looked around at others. I saw people sitting upright through times of prayer or meditation who were clearly deep in it. I have always been good at faking it, but I knew that I was just putting on a mask. I wanted to move. I wanted to scream with frustration – 'Why isn't this working for me?!' There must be something wrong with me, I thought. I felt like a fraud.

I needed to admit that this is linked to the way my brain works. I cannot sit still, I fidget, my brain needs constant stimulation and chases after physical sensations. Occupying this body of mine for 33 years, I am still learning how it functions. It has been suggested to me by my GP and by some other people that I might actually be somewhere on the neurodivergent spectrum, although it has not been confirmed by a specialist. Nonetheless, this suggestion alone turned out to be the turning point in the way that I think of my own spiritual practice. I recognised that I need to actively engage my physical senses to help me harness my attention. One way of putting it is to say that I need 'bells and smells' in my spiritual practice ... at least to some extent.

I discovered that brewing a strong and fragrant cup of tea, which I can hold, smell, and taste as I meditate, helps my concentration. Walking a labyrinth is great too. So is slipping mala beads or rosary beads through my fingers as I pray or count breaths. The 'Knitting Club' at our General Assembly's annual meetings comes to mind – busy hands, focused minds. I decided to fully embrace this part of me and experiment with engaging my physicality as my spiritual resource.

In our Unitarian tradition, there is an emphasis on the rational mind, on thinking, and on words. After all, our denomination came to prominence during the Enlightenment – the period of time in human history when the faculty of reason was perceived to be at the pinnacle of what it means to be human. *Cogito, ergo sum* – I think, therefore I am. This primacy of logic and reason was so prominent that it is even self-evident in the architecture of many of our chapels, where the pulpit – a place for the spoken word – often occupies the central spot.

Theologically, this approach can be described as *cataphatic* – we only know and worship God through the use of affirmative statements, God is so great that we must keep on talking and thinking about him/her/them/it. I began to wonder whether, since stillness and the spoken word tire me, I should embrace their opposites – movements and feelings. I realised that walks in green spaces have always been spiritually nourishing for me, so I decided to approach movement more seriously. I decided to try the *apophatic* way, devoid of words, as nothing that we can say or write about God can possibly be sufficient. Words and thoughts are so limited. Such apophatic method, starved of words, but rooted in physical movement, became my personal practice, my way of recharging and sustaining myself so that I could then come back to people: to the world of words, thoughts, and concepts.

What I do to nourish my soul varies from day to day. It could be anything from the unceremonious and apparently profane, for example cardio exercises or weight workouts, through swimming and walks in nature, to yoga and tai chi. I engage in some form of meditation through movement at least once a day. Some days I do it alone, sometimes with other people. I set the intention of simply feeling fully alive and being truly present in my body in that moment. In the words of the American Unitarian Universalist minister Gretchen Haley,[5] I 'give up the fight for some other moment, some other life than here and now. Give up the longing for some other world, the wishing for other choices to make. I surrender only to this life, this day, this hour.' I focus on the rhythms of my breath, and my heart beating in unison with my chosen music. I pay attention to my chest rising as it expands, filled with oxygen. I start from precisely where I find myself, giving up the desire to change anything, be anything, or achieve anything. I simply observe myself and notice my place in the world of which I am part. I set no intention; I let go of expectations. Any outcomes of this simplest prayer will arrive (or not) of their own accord, be it praise, lament, a feeling of oneness, solace, bliss, or peace. My every breath anchors me in my incarnate reality, stripped of the comforting blankets of words and ideas. There is a power in the apparent vulnerability of the naked mind, undressed of all expectations, wants, and ideas. With nothing to hide and nowhere to run, the only possible strategy is to simply 'be' – with honesty, vulnerability, and trust. Then, my heartbeats can propel my awareness deeper into the perfection of this inner Eden of mine.

I completely give in to all these physical sensations with feelings of gratitude: to every beat of my heart, every beat of the music hitting my ear drums, every movement of my chest, every muscle shaking, every drop of sweat running down my skin. I feel as if through movement I can experience the Divine Reality in a way that is not accessible to me through language or cold, rational thinking. Embracing my physicality,

---

5   Adapted from *Surrender to This Life* by Gretchen Haley on the UUA Worship Web: https://www.uua.org/worship/words/opening/surrender-life

this gift that we have been given, these body-clothes, enables me to feel at one not only with myself but also with the whole Universe. I have had several experiences that one may call mystical, although I understand if it sounds strange for the sceptics among you. But every time it happened, every time I have had moments of deep spiritual significance, my mind was at rest and my body was engaged.

I am utterly unable to describe the Divine without resorting to negative descriptions of this Ultimate Reality. I do not know who or what God is, but I am convinced that I cannot know God – I can only feel God. I do not know where God resides, but I doubt that God is in lines of ink on the paper, or in human concepts or constructs. Any attempts to find God through intellectual wrestling, or arguments, or persuasions are, in my view, also futile. My instinct is to give up on trying to know or discern God through logic and reckoning, trusting that we, all of us, already have the ability to use our emotions and feelings to tap into that great mystery which cannot be known, but can be felt. We only need to become receptive, feeling, experiencing, and listening to the loving voice arising out of nothingness, speaking without words, but coming across in the rhymes – of music, of breath, of heartbeat, the hum of a singing bowl; blending the limits of time with eternity, and the limits of space with infinity. This is the language which cannot be understood by brain alone but can be experienced by the fullness of our being.

In other words, for me, God starts where language begins to fail. Through physical movement I allow myself simply to exist in the very moment. This not only enables me to feel grounded but also fills me with enthusiasm for life. By 'enthusiasm' I mean the state of bliss and tranquillity that emerges from recognition of having our being 'in God's essence', from the Greek word *enthusiasmos* – literally meaning 'in God's essence'. To quote Julian of Norwich: 'mine understanding took that our Substance is in God'. This, in turn, enables me to abandon the chase for some other life, some other goal, and to relinquish aspirations to be anything other than who I am now. I no longer see my life through the metaphor of a journey which aims to arrive at a certain destination. I see it as a dance – a movement through time and space which is to be savoured in *the now*.

Partly it was this realisation that pushed me to qualify as an exercise instructor. When I am not serving as a Minister, I can be spotted at local gyms teaching BODYATTACK™ (a high-energy and high-impact aerobics and sports training), BODYPUMP™ (a strength and resistance training using barbells and weight plates), and BODYBALANCE™ (an amalgamation of Yoga, Tai Chi, and Pilates, creating a sense of relaxation and serenity). None of these classes is explicitly spiritual, and yet they are my spiritual practice. And since many of my students know what my day job is, I have had some of the most fascinating spiritual conversations at gyms. Sometimes deeper than in church buildings.

I keep reminding people attending my classes that if they have goals in mind – i.e. losing weight, becoming fitter, stronger, or whatever – that's all good. But the point of a class should be to enjoy the moment. The point of the class is the class. Just as in the Rule of St Benedict, it is about the time spent on an activity, rather than any potential achievement *per se*. It is the dance in the moment that matters: there is no special destination to arrive at. And most importantly, my gym-class mantra is that we exercise not because we hate our bodies, but because we love them.

Engaging with movement and with my physicality on a deeper level, much to my surprise, turned out to be an incredibly rich spiritual resource – a font of peace and tranquillity, helping me, in turn, to minister to others. Most of my ideas for Sunday services come to me while exercising. And since the classes that I teach are done to music, we have no choice but to get out of our heads, trust in our bodies, feel how incredible they are, synchronise our movements and breathing patterns. The sense of oneness that this induces is profound, created in an unlikely place – a gym. *Bodyfulness = joyfulness.*

PART FOUR – Laura

Two contemporary women writers introduced me to the concept of 'bodyfulness', which has revolutionised how I approach my embodied spiritual practice: Christine Caldwell and Christine Valters Paintner.

In her book, *Bodyfulness*,[6] Christine Caldwell writes of the body as an experience rather than a possession, and defines bodyfulness as conscious engagement with and acceptance of the embodied self, leading to right action towards lessening suffering and increasing potential.

Caldwell explores what she terms the four pillars of bodyfulness practice: breathing, sensing, moving, and relating, as well as exploring issues of body identity, body authority, and body stories. She suggests various exercises to try, but also emphasises that bodyfulness is embedded in our everyday experience. She concludes:

> Embedded practice may be another good synonym for bodyfulness. How we reach out and pick up our child, how we wait before eating to check to see if we are really hungry, how we gaze at a troubled stranger, how we notice a gut feeling, and how we breathe into a happy moment – all these experiences can be bodyful. We access this bodyful state by practicing right now, during this breath, feeling this sensation, noticing this small motion. Right here. Right now.

Christine Valters Paintner, in her book, *The Wisdom of the Body*,[7] takes the reader on a contemplative journey of the body, exploring viriditas, breath, senses, emotions, thoughts, vulnerability, incarnation, joy, earthliness, and coming home. She writes that, for her, bodyfulness means exploring the wilderness of the body, listening for how it wants to be nourished with food, movement, breath, deep rest, and delighting in the presence of the divine in the pleasures of the senses.

Bodyfulness inspired me to consider that my spiritual practice need not be just a set of exercises that I do in the morning, but I could be paying attention to and reflecting upon how I am in myself and in my relationships with others.

---

6   Christine Caldwell: *Bodyfulness: Somatic Practices for Presence, Empowerment, and Waking Up in This Life* (Shambhala Publications, Boulder, Colorado, 2018).

7   Christine Valters Paintner: *The Wisdom of the Body: A Contemplative Journey to Wholeness for Women* (Ave Maria Press, Notre Dame, Indiana, 2017).

Paying attention to and reflecting upon my everyday embodied experience – how I feel when I laugh with a friend, or play with my dog, how my shoulders drop and my breathing slows when I enter the woods, how I discern with my gut whether to say Yes or No, how I listen to the signals from my body that tell me when I need to rest, how I hold eye-contact when I speak words of encouragement or nod in acknowledgement of someone else's pain, how I felt myself smiling and my heart expanding with joy when I saw a young girl cartwheeling along the platform as I got off the tram yesterday – all these things I can now frame as spiritual practice; they contribute to my wholeness and well-being, and the wholeness and well-being of others with whom I come into contact.

I am learning to become ever more fully present in my embodied experience, even when that experience is uncomfortable and painful, even on the days when I feel grief deep in my bones. I am gaining a deeper appreciation of my body as the ground of my being. As the Psalmist says, 'I praise You, for I am awesomely, wondrously made'.[8] I am gaining a deeper understanding of my faith that the universe is the body of God, and, as St Paul says, we are all members of that body, who care for each other as members of one body, suffering with and rejoicing with one another.

Rabbi Rachel Barenblat, in her blog, *The Velveteen Rabbi*,[9] explores the story in the Book of Exodus about the Israelites escaping from slavery in Egypt by crossing the Sea of Reeds (mistranslated as the Red Sea in the King James Version). She also ponders on a commentary on that passage by Rabbi Shalom Noach Barzovsky, who teaches:

> there are three kinds of *emunah* (elemental trust): trusting mind, trusting heart, and trusting body. And the highest of these is *emunat ha-evarim*, trusting with one's limbs, where deep trust penetrates every fibre of one's being. In that moment of leaping [into the Sea of

----

8   Psalm 139, verse 14.
9   https://velveteenrabbi.blogs.com/blog/2009/04/song-for-the-seventh-day.html

Reeds] the children of Israel trusted fully in the One, and therefore the holy spirit rested upon them and sang in them and song burst forth not only from their lips but in their very limbs.

Barenblat comments: 'Trusting with one's body: what a radical notion. Not just trusting one's body (which is challenging enough, sometimes) – but trusting with the body ... Taking that plunge, and being transformed by it ... May we open ourselves to the transformative possibilities of walking through the world with eyes made for wonder.'

Paul Simon sang, 'These are the days of miracle and wonder.' I give thanks for the miracle and wonder of the matter that makes up my body, your body, the earth. Trusting Life, trusting with the body, trusting that a leap of faith will lead to liberation, feeling the invitation and the response in my body – that's what bodyfulness means for me.

PART FIVE – Arek

One of my most profound experiences of using breath as spiritual practice occurred at Mill Hill Chapel in Leeds. Before the pandemic lockdown a group of Sikhs working in the city centre used the chapel for their mid-week lunch-time Simran meditation. And everyone was invited to join in, so I did, on several occasions. Simran meditation is meditation on breath – the life force – in which you chant the Sikh name of God: *Waheguru. Guru* is someone who leads you from the dark to light; *Wahe* means wondrous, magnificent, or literally WOW! *The WOW!-Guru: God.* Meditating, we inhaled as we said 'wahe', and exhaled as we said 'guru'. Each meditation session consisted of just under half an hour of uninterrupted chanting. There was no leader in the group, and yet, as we collectively chanted, we found ourselves speeding up, slowing down, getting louder and quieter in unison. We went with the flow, tapping into our instincts and feelings. In the most wonderful way we connected with one another, and with the universe, in one breath, one chant, one resounding sound, one heartbeat.

PART SIX – Laura

One of the most accessible ways in which we can ground ourselves in the present moment and in our bodies is through our breath. 'The Lord God formed man from the dust of the earth. He blew into his nostrils the breath of life, and man became a living being' (Genesis 2:7). The Jewish Study Bible commentary on this verse reads:

> Here, man has a lowlier origin than in the parallel in 1: 26–28. He is created not in the image of God but from the dust of the earth. But he also has a closer and more intimate relationship with his Creator, who blows the breath of life into him, transforming that lowly, earth-bound creature into a living being. In this understanding, the human being is not an amalgam of perishable body and immortal soul, but a psychophysical unity who depends on God for life itself.

Hildegard's version of this text, from her own vision of creation, is even more earthy:

> With my mouth I kiss my own chosen creation. I uniquely, lovingly, embrace every image I have made out of the earth's clay. With a fiery spirit I transform it into a body to serve all the world.[10]

Hildegard had a very strong sense that a human being is 'a psychophysical unity who depends on God for life itself'. She had a very strong sense of the sacredness of the body and the earth, and of the whole of life being held in divine love. In the West we are used to thinking in a dualistic manner – body and soul, mind and matter – but the word 'Ruach' in Hebrew means breath, wind, and spirit. It refers to things both physical and more-than-physical, the tangible and the intangible, which are all

---

10 Quoted in Gabriele Uhlein, *Meditations with Hildegard of Bingen* (Bear and Company, Rochester, Vermont, 2001).

part of the same reality. The breath, which is in a very physical sense our life-force, is both tangible and intangible. We feel it but we cannot see it – except on a very cold day! Most of the time we are unaware of our own breathing: it is something that we do automatically. Since 2020, the airborne transmission of coronavirus has made us all painfully aware of the negative consequences of the fact that we are all breathing the same air. But it is also a sacred sign of our interconnectedness, and today I would like to invite us into a conscious, sacred relationship with the breath in our own bodies as the life-force, our connection to the One Source of Life that we share.

I am inspired by these words of the herbalist and poet Brigit Anna McNeill, writing in a Facebook post:[11]

> Reciprocity is in each moment, invisible threads of connection that support and nurture. Take the simple act of breathing. We breathe out carbon dioxide, which the trees, plants and seaweeds love and need. They breathe us in, the very essence that moved through us, holding stories of blood, grief, joy and bone, now moves through them. Turning our breath into oxygen, they transform what we let go of into the support we need to survive and thrive. As we breathe in, the very essence that moved in tree, plant and ocean, holding stories of wildness, salt, earth, roots, tides and growth, now moves in us. Each breath full of the strength of oak, the tenacity of weed, the magic of foxglove, the depths of sea and the alchemy of earth.

Hildegard referred to herself as 'a feather on the breath of God'. To share that feeling, to know that I am supported and directed by the Source of Life, I need to give myself space to tune into it. One of the best ways I have found to do that is to rest my awareness in my heart-space and feel the calming rhythm of the resting breath as the life-force moving through my body, and through the world.

---

11   https://www.facebook.com/anna.b.mcneill/posts/.

The Sufi scholar Neil Douglas-Klotz, in his wonderful book, *Prayers of the Cosmos*,[12] writes about the many layers of meaning in the Aramaic Lord's Prayer. For each line of the prayer he suggests some accompanying body-prayer practices. I opened the book at random the other day and read, 'While lying or sitting, return to the peaceful place inside, creating by feeling your heartbeat and breathing. As the medieval mystic Hildegard of Bingen said, everything may be felt a "feather on the breath of God".' A lovely moment of synchronicity.

Of course it is not just in the Judaeo-Christian tradition that breath is considered sacred and synonymous with life-force, or spirit. Dating back 3,000 years, Indian sacred texts talk of 'prana' or 'life-force' or 'vital energy', from which we get 'pranayama' or 'controlled breathing' – an integral part of ancient yoga techniques and still practised today in both Eastern and Western yoga traditions. In China, the life-force was known as 'chi', most often translated as 'energy'. The Chinese system of conscious breathing is known as 'qigong', or 'breath-work'. Managing the flow of 'prana' or 'chi' in the body became the basis of ancient Indian and Chinese medicine.

This brings me to the fourth inspirational person: James Nestor and his recent book, *Breath*,[13] which goes into great detail about various research studies on breathing, from ancient sacred texts to scientific studies of the twenty-first century. He also explores a variety of controlled breathing techniques. He concludes that the perfect breath is through the nose, inhaling and exhaling for 5.5–6 seconds each way. This just happens to be the same rhythm as many mantras – for example, *'om mani padme hum'* in the Buddhist tradition, or *'sa ta na ma'* in the Kundalini Yoga tradition. It is also the same pattern as the Latin version of the *Ave Maria* prayer of the Catholic rosary. These ancient prayers are designed to be chanted at the optimum number of breaths per minute, to promote feelings of calmness and well-being.

------

12   Neil Douglas-Klotz, *Prayers of the Cosmos: Meditations on the Aramaic Words of Jesus* (Harper, San Francisco, 1994).
13   James Nestor, *Breath: The New Science of a Lost Art* (Riverhead Books, New York City, 2020).

Hildegard says that prayer is 'breathing in and breathing out the one breath of the universe'. What does it feel like in our bodies when we breathe as a sacred act, when the breath itself becomes our prayer? Breathing in and breathing out the one breath of the universe. In a Blessing written by Hildegard and translated by Gabriele Uhlein,[14]

Good people,
most royal greening verdancy,
rooted in the sun,
you shine with radiant light.
In this circle of earthly existence,
you shine so finely,
it surpasses understanding,
God hugs you.
You are encircled
by the arms
of the mystery of God.

Questions for Reflection and Discussion

1. How do you feel about embodied spirituality and the idea of 'bodyfulness'? Would you, or do you, engage in a 'bodyful' spiritual practice?

2. Does your congregation offer varied styles of worship, including worship practices for people like Arek and Laura, for whom the most authentic form of spiritual practice is to engage with the body?

3. Do you agree with the suggestion that striving for right relationship with one's physical self can translate into developing right relationship with others and the wider web of existence?

---

14   Gabriele Uhlein, *Meditations with Hildegard of Bingen* (Bear and Company, Rochester, Vermont, 2001).

The authors

Revd Arek Malecki is the minister of the Great Meeting Unitarian Chapel in Leicester by day, and a group exercise instructor by night. He grew up as a member of the Roman Catholic Church in Poland, and began his Unitarian journey at Mill Hill Chapel in Leeds, where he had been a member for several years before deciding to pursue his call to Unitarian ministry. Arek trained for ministry with the Unitarian College and studied Theology at Luther King Centre in Manchester. His dissertation, entitled 'Mystic Sweat: Unveiling Spiritual Dimensions of Music-infused Workout Classes and their Implications for Ministry', suggests that for some people physical and sensory engagement is one of the most effective ways of getting in touch with their deepest selves, while choreography, together with carefully selected music, can contribute to the creation of a quasi-liturgical experience. When not at the church or the gym, he can often be found hiking in the countryside.

Revd Laura Dobson is the part-time minister with Chorlton Unitarians and part-time co-minister with the Unitarian Transformers community-building project. Laura discovered the Unitarian movement in 2013 and began attending Chorlton Unitarian Church, becoming Lay Person in Charge in 2016. She completed her ministry training in 2021. She studied for a BA then MA in Theology and Religious Studies at the University of Leeds in the 1990s. Laura is passionate about embodied spirituality and eco-spirituality, and draws inspiration from medieval women mystics such as Hildegard von Bingen. She enjoys daily walks in the woods with her border collie, loves to sing, and sporadically practises yoga.

4 Being in Right Relationship with Those Who Diverge from Assumed Social Norms

Tor Glinwell and Alex Brianson

Introduction

In this chapter we want to think about how, as Unitarians, we can be in right relationship with people who are different from ourselves, including those who don't fit the assumed norms of the society that we all live in. Some of these norms are usually unspoken, and simply taken as read – for example, the belief that everyone is able-bodied and in good health, has no neurological difference, and is heterosexual and cisgender. Such assumptions are a form of discrimination and may be both deliberate and prejudiced (for example, trans-phobia or homo-phobia) or simply the result of a lack of conscious thought (such as assuming that everyone can access a building without the provision of a ramp at the entrance).

For several decades now, feminists have protested against the unspoken assumption that the male is the norm. In Alex's former career, for example, there were unspoken assumptions, even ten years ago, that employees could work 80 hours a week because they had someone else to take care of the kids and the home. We will focus here on three aspects of divergence from assumed norms:

- being non-heterosexual and, in Tor's case, identifying as transgender;
- neurodiversity – in our cases, autism and Attention-Deficit Hyperactivity Disorder (ADHD), for Alex and Tor respectively;
- living with disability and chronic illness.

We intend to draw on our personal experience as Unitarians, and our core message is that *seeking to be in right relationship with those who diverge from assumed social norms is an on-going commitment, not a one-off gesture.* People change over time in what they know about themselves, or how their bodies function; for instance, after his diagnosis of autism at the age of 48, Alex has been on a continuing mission to understand himself better in ways that would not have occurred to him previously.

We assume as a starting point that Unitarians may have a head start in being in right relationship with those living in the margins, because many of us in the denomination consciously chose our progressive religion and honestly wish for radical social change. But we also hold that in order to make this a reality, Unitarians can be hamstrung when meeting 'others' on their terms, because most of our congregations are not very diverse, or perhaps are not *visibly* diverse. This means that we need actively to prioritise being in right relationship with those who are different from us, and regularly seek their input into how we as individuals and as congregations can do better.

We will present three case studies, concerning gender and/or sexuality difference, neurodiversity, and living with chronic illness and/or disability. Before we begin our contribution, however, we want to acknowledge a couple of important points about where we ourselves start in all this, and what our own limitations are.

First, in keeping with the concept of intersectionality developed by the US scholar and activist Kimberlé Crenshaw, we both know that, for all our marginalisation, we too benefit from forms of privilege, and there are limits to our awareness of how the lives of 'others' can be affected by their divergence from assumed norms: Alex is a white, cisgender, gay man in a heterosexist and still racist and patriarchal society, and Tor is a white, queer, transgender person. So our point is not that we have perfect vision and practice, but rather that our experiences in life as 'different' Unitarians may help all of us think about what it means to be in right relationship with each other. We know there will be other Unitarians in the same marginal groups as us whose experiences differ from ours, and we don't claim to be all-knowing about what it is like to be members of those groups as Unitarians. We just want to draw on our lived experiences to speak authentically.

Second, we very much like the notion expressed by Jane Blackall and Sarah Tinker that being in right relationship requires curiosity, being interested in people who are in some way 'other' from ourselves, and seeking to apply the Platinum Rule of *treating people as they would wish to be treated.* That has been our guiding thought in preparing our contribution to this volume of Summer School theme talks.

Gender and sexual orientation

This section begins with a little story. Tor married his spouse Cheryl while still presenting as a non-binary person. Having moved to Norwich, they attended Norwich Pride, where they met the local Unitarians and marched with them, promising that they would be back to join them in the chapel. But the pressures of the house move meant that they did not attend a service until Easter Sunday the next year – a full eight months later. At their first Sunday service in their new community, the then-Chair announced the following in the weekly notices as part of the introduction to the day's service: 'We have a wedding on Friday, so there's no parking, and actually it's lovely to see Rachel and Melissa here, whose wedding blessing we will be celebrating.' Rachel and Melissa were not present, and it was an innocent mistake, but to Tor and Cheryl it was a bit of a *whoops* moment, indicating that to the speaker all apparently same-sex couples perhaps look interchangeable. In that moment the Chairperson probably thought they were doing something lovely by welcoming a new couple to the community, and their intention was indeed laudable; but, while the speaker might have assumed that it was a minor error to get the names wrong, such a mistake can carry more weight for the people concerned, who might be hurt by the mistake and the apparent assumptions behind it. Fortunately, Tor and Cheryl were already Unitarians, but for a complete newcomer that instance might have indicated that there was no great recognition of queer people in the chapel community, and they would need to continue searching for a spiritual home. Additionally, calling attention to individuals in such a way can be fraught with risk, because not everyone enjoys the spotlight, and they may find that level of attention off-putting.

Luckily, the chapel concerned has proved that it has an ongoing commitment to the diverse LGBTQ+ community by continuing to attend every Pride event which has been put on in Norwich over the past 14 years, sometimes hosting extra events during Pride Week, especially during the campaign for equal marriage, as well as having hosted numerous blessings, weddings, and ceremonies for LGBTQ+ couples over the years.

But that does not mean that the need for such work is over. There is always room for change or different approaches, so the chapel recently took the step of initiating an informal evening once a month, with hot drinks and cakes served in the hall, aptly named 'LGBTQ+ Coffee and Cake'. It was clearly stated that the space would be alcohol-free, because there were already plenty of opportunities for drinking within the wider queer community, and not serving alcohol makes it a safe space for those who don't (or don't want to) drink alcohol. The chapel did this to acknowledge that there is a greater statistical likelihood of substance misuse in the group with whom they are aiming to make a connection: a point that might have been missed without LGBTQ+ people being involved in the organisation of the event. And it should be noted that this is not an event that aims to evangelise about LGBTQ+ Unitarianism, or even about spirituality more generally. Rather, it is using the resources at the chapel's disposal to host a space for friends to meet for conversation and connection. If someone who attends the event then decides to try out a service or other congregational opportunity, that's great, but it is not the focus of the evening. Inclusion work through outreach is best done for its own sake.

In terms of spiritual issues, there does need to be a greater mindfulness of the needs of queer people when hosting Unitarian events, like a carol service or a concert, where it might be assumed that it is appropriate to assign elements according to assumed gender. For example, in the carol *Good King Wenceslas* there are verses which will traditionally be sung by Gentlemen rather than Ladies, and of course also vice versa – whereas in musical terms what we actually want people to hear together is high and low voices, and trans people's voices may not sound the same as those of cisgender people. So use the terms 'high and low voices' instead of a gender binary if it is absolutely essential to the aesthetic of your event; this small change of phrasing could make all the difference to a congregation member or visitor who maybe finds Christmas a hard time anyway. Certainly nothing is lost by being inclusive in this way.

Queer people have been excluded from spiritual life in many religions, times, and cultures, and although we ourselves have not always been treated in this way, the fact that we have so often been rendered invisible, or used as objects of scorn and hatred, by religious folk often makes us turn against religion altogether. Sometimes this discrimination has been deliberate: just ask the Church of England about the LGBTQ+ clergy who are forced to enter into celibate marriages, when no such commitment applies to heterosexual clergy. Sometimes the discrimination has been inadvertent; for instance, Kittredge Cherry's Q Spirit work shows how a lack of cultural knowledge on the part of translators of the Bible means that we don't always get the full picture of the world in which Jesus lived. For example, the Centurion who, in Greek versions of the New Testament, asks Jesus to heal his 'pais' and is told by Jesus that he is a model of faith, is asking Jesus to heal a man who is his lover, not just his servant, and Jesus would have known this.[1] So better translations and knowledge of history can make us feel included where currently we don't appear to exist.

The same is true of the versions of Greek myths or other religions that are taught in mainstream UK schools, because kids don't need to know about all that nasty queer stuff, do they? Did you know, for instance, that Dionysus is what we would call bisexual? That many other deities of the ancients, as well as those of other religions still considered mainstream in particular places had (or have) gender-variant priests and priestesses? Were you taught that Erzulie, the Voudou goddess of love, beauty, arts, and the sensual realm, manifests as both male and female, and as cisgender and transgender, and as heterosexual, lesbian, *and* gay? It usually takes queer people years to find all this out, if indeed we ever do. How lovely it would have been for both of us to see ourselves

---

1   Luke 7, verses 1–10 and Matthew 8 verses 5–13.

explicitly and happily reflected in the dominant understandings of the Divine around us while we were growing up.

So if Unitarians want to reach out to non-cisgender and heterosexual people, this requires a willingness to adapt existing ways of thinking, working, and being. It is about allowing us to be our full selves without having to sanitise or adapt our lives for the benefit of straight people. For those of us who are trans, non-binary, asexual, or aromantic, queering Unitarianism by making us welcome in all our diversity and difference would bring greater justice and security into our lives. Some people's identity and sexual orientation defy labels that expect them to be permanently one thing or another, and if we can build a religious tradition that actively honours and includes people who live beyond the male/female and heterosexual/homosexual binaries, that would be very welcome. It could also help us as a denomination to sit more comfortably alongside certain other non-Western religions which often see our dominant social norms of sex and gender as reductive.

Neurodiversity

Being autistic has shaped Alex's life since he was born, of course, but he only received his diagnosis at the age of 48 and has learned much more about the condition since then. The fact that there are so many points on the autism spectrum means that how it is for him may not be quite how it is for anyone else, but his strong ethical sense, special interests (what other people sometimes call 'obsessions'), love for structure and guidelines and rules, hyper-empathy, deep emotions, and precision with language are good examples of common autistic traits.

Some of these characteristics dovetail nicely with Unitarianism. Alex has a special interest in theology, which comes in handy, and his refusal automatically to accept the edicts of a person in authority just because they have the right title sits pretty well with the Nonconformist history of the denomination. His love of language and its exact usage can make him a good communicator. And his hyper-empathy makes him want to help others who are suffering.

But such hyper-empathy can also be disabling, by creating a tendency to be overwhelmed. There is so much to be distressed by in the world, and far more suffering than any of us can individually remedy. This can lead to mental-health problems, and/or the need to retreat to a quiet place on his own for a period of time. Alex's reliance upon his rational mind to understand everything, because more instinctive ways of knowing are alien or imperceptible to him, can make him unable instinctively to access the more symbolic or ritual aspects of spiritual life. And the anxiety generated by being in a world or community whose norms he does not necessarily understand can be crippling as well as exhausting.

Tor's neurodivergence means that he found writing his parts of this contribution difficult, because his brain resists doing things until the last minute, and sometimes not even then, which is galling, because there is another part of him that is a perfectionist. His medical diagnosis, ADHD (attention-deficit hyperactivity disorder), is a terrible name for what is actually a chronic dopamine deficiency affecting the functioning of the frontal lobe of the brain, which manifests in many fascinating and often frustrating ways. Certainly, he does not suffer from a lack of capacity to pay attention; what actually happens is that his brain tries to pay attention to everything all at once...

After being diagnosed as a child, Tor's ability to manage sitting still and working in school generally improved, as is common for people with ADHD, and this is one of the reasons why some people still see the condition as a childhood disorder that people grow out of. In fact, what happens is that the symptoms on which the diagnosis was made may not persist, but are overtaken by other behaviours, such as impulsivity and hyper-focusing on things that provide that dopamine hit, only to move swiftly on to something else.

So your congregation member with ADHD will be the one who generally has brilliant ideas but struggles to complete them. Or maybe they are enthusiastic in person when you broach something with them, but three unanswered emails later you are wondering if they are truly the right person for the project. This is where teamwork is essential. They may want to take charge of your chapel library, for example, but they might also need a buddy – not to do the job, but to sit with them while they rearrange and catalogue the books. People with ADHD often make brilliant archivists, if given the right support. For example, Tor's spouse is frequently stunned when he can find with pinpoint accuracy places that he has not visited for many years.

Disability and chronic illness

Having Chronic Fatigue Syndrome (often abbreviated to CFS, and also called ME or Myalgic Encephalomyelitis) has affected every part of Alex's life, including the spiritual ones. It is an illness that consumes the sufferer's energy, and often brings significant pain and sensory overload problems too. It is hard to treat, has no agreed cause, and can go away completely if you are lucky – or worsen to the point where you can't get out of bed for years. It can even kill you by wasting away your body and making it impossible to eat or move. He is learning to live with it, but finds the process very challenging, because treatment requires the unlearning of so many behaviours and accepting the extreme vulnerability that goes with not knowing how much he will be able to do on any given day.

His horizons have shrunk considerably, and all decisions that he makes are now both intrinsically more complicated because of the chronic illness dimension and harder to make because of the brain fog and shortened attention span that CFS brings. Alex used to write multi-disciplinary academic books based on years of original research. Now he struggles to read anything other than fiction, and sometimes is unable to do that. It can be lonely, and also a source of shame and disappointment. He finds it very hard to push past the sense of diminishment, of unworthiness, because even if he knows that people would not necessarily see him that way, he himself did, and sometimes still does, despite a shed load of therapy.

This has obviously shaped his life as a Unitarian. On the negative side, it makes him less able to be active in the community, even remotely. For instance, he signed up for the Unitarian–Hindu engagement group, but left it as he was embarrassed by not being able to attend the online meetings: they were in the evening, and often he cannot concentrate enough at that time of the day. He finds himself taking a peripheral role in the community, which is a great difference from his life before CFS arrived. More positively, part of the treatment plan for his condition is to reduce the levels of stress in his life, so he spends far more time meditating or in deep relaxation than before, and this has made his everyday living more consciously spiritual.

If you had asked Tor as a young child if he was, or considered himself, disabled, he would have said no, of course not. But he had (and still has) eczema, which involved being treated with various creams that often made him scream because of his extreme skin sensitivity. He had to avoid most bubble baths, soaps, and even his friend's dogs. But in his first year at university he had an experience that changed his perspective.

He studied psychology, and was required to join the school's pool of semi-willing participants in research. As part of this, he did a test which involved measuring galvanic skin response to an electrical current, delivered by a little meter worn on one finger while completing the set task. An electrical current passed across already sensitive skin and, on top of the probable stress of his first year at university, managing his own studies and living away from home, triggered an infection. Suddenly what had just seemed a bodily quirk which had been annoying to manage as a child could affect his studies: he could not take notes in lectures. The flat that he shared had a door knob, rather than a handle, and the soft cotton gloves that the doctor suggested to protect his skin meant that he could not easily open the door. He wanted lasagne for dinner at the pub but could not use both a knife and fork, so his sister had to cut up the pasta sheets for him. It was a very formative experience for him in terms of his identity as disabled, showing how an illness or condition that is seemingly limited in its impact can in fact become extremely debilitating, making him feel able to lay claim to a part of himself that he had not truly acknowledged before.

After that experience, he was very much more open with others about what his health needs are in regards to his health. Over the years, he has been diagnosed with various other allergies that can have an impact on his life and his ability to take part in everyday activities. This is a good example of how disabilities may not be visible to others but have a big impact on the person in question, making group activities very difficult or even impossible to tolerate. For instance, Tor's allergy to latex means that his presence at a chapel service that included a naming ceremony featuring a beautiful balloon arch as part of the decoration would cause a health problem for him. To manage this kind of circumstance, it is vital to have proper communication, for instance including a message to a congregation's mailing list telling people that there is this particular feature in your Sunday service. The same applies, of course, to food needs; it can be lovely to have bring-and-share lunches, or maybe to have a hospitality team who take care of group catering, but some people will need a heads-up that food is involved in that day's gathering, so that they can make arrangements for their own catering, or even if necessary leave directly after the service if there is too great a risk of anaphylactic shock from some of the food. This may mean that people with particular food needs feel excluded from these community gatherings, so checking-in with them in advance about how they can be included is a good idea.

A final issue in this section is about considering the needs of those who are physically disabled – beyond installing a ramp to enable access to your building. Many of us in Unitarian congregations pride ourselves on having beautiful historic buildings. But how many of those buildings have lectern or pulpits which are inaccessible to those who use physical mobility devices such as rollators, and manual and powered wheelchairs? Would such a person be able to lead worship easily? Would they be able to move around easily once in the building, accessing all the necessary facilities?

Conclusions

Being in right relationship with those whose lives are different from those considered normative in our society is an on-going process that will evolve alongside the congregation and its individual members. It is a long-haul commitment, not a one-off gesture, and everyone stands both to learn and to benefit from it. We have ourselves learned how to be more inclusive over time, not least because our own lives have changed and uncovered issues that we had not experienced before. We also recognise that there are always likely to be ways in which our Unitarian congregations can improve our denomination's ability to be genuine places of equal inclusion. It is likely that certain congregations have already amassed much useful experience and understanding concerning particular questions of expanding inclusion that could very helpfully be shared with others.

The other contributors to this collection of theme talks focus on aspects of inclusivity and right relationship that complement our focus here, and we happily acknowledge that they have suggestions and experiences that we could usefully learn from. As a result, we want to end with a set of suggestions about ways to include queer, neurodivergent, and disabled /chronically ill people more fully in Unitarian life. We don't see them as a check-list to guarantee being in right relationship with marginalised members of the congregation, but they are a good starting point, and they draw on our own experiences, which means that we can vouch for their helpfulness. They are listed as bullet points below.

- Do an audit of congregational needs every year. Are there ways of including others that have not been tried? Are there potential problems in communication or delivery style that have not been identified?
- Ask congregation members who are 'different' to help leaders and the community understand what they need, but don't make them responsible for educating you once the need is identified: do your own research.
- Actively choose service material that reflects non-mainstream lives, for instance exploring LGBTQ faces of the Divine, or how disability affects a person's spiritual life.
- Don't assume that everyone feels able to make spoken contributions in services or church meetings. Make internet chat functions or anonymous suggestion boxes available.
- Be mindful of social anxiety and how people may like to be included – or left on their own.
- Be mindful of the potential for sensory overload or inability to concentrate for long periods of time on something that is only heard rather than read, and moderate your meetings, services, or worship materials accordingly.

- Be aware that emotions generated by material in services may be felt much more keenly than you imagine, in terms of both happiness and distress, but may not be identifiable to the person in question until much later on – which may well have implications for pastoral care of the congregation.

Questions for Reflection and Discussion

1. Do you know which barriers to full inclusion in your church community are experienced by members of your congregation?

2. What arrangements has your congregation made to ensure that members from marginalised groups can express their needs? From the point of view of the marginalised groups themselves, how effective are those arrangements, and how can they be improved?

3. How does your congregation incorporate material (in chapel services and other activities) that explicitly speaks to the lives of marginalised groups?

The authors

Alex Brianson is a member of Kensington Unitarians and Wirral Unitarians. He lives in Birkenhead and is a retired academic turned novelist. He is autistic and also lives with Myalgic Encephalomyelitis / Chronic Fatigue Syndrome (ME/CFS).

Tor Glinwell is a Unitarian, originally from Dudley in the West Midlands and now resident in the beautiful and radical town of Norwich in Norfolk. He is a trans man, proudly queer and neurodivergent. He studied psychology and for the last 18 years has worked in education.

5 Right Relationship, Racism, and Reparations

Winnie Gordon

What I love about Summer School is the sharing of lived experience, interspersed with theological thought and common sense. Speakers give with open-heartedness, and participants embrace with wonder. I have experienced wonder all this week: thank you, fellow speakers. I hope that tonight you can all accept Cody and me, openly sharing our lived experiences and encouraging you to engage with the world outside this space.

Every loving parent prays for their child to make it home safely every time the child steps outside the door. It is a prayer that is common to all humanity, regardless of colour, creed, or kind. And I don't wish to detract from that. But I must add that people of colour may feel such fear even more intensely, and pray a little harder, as they know the added dangers of racial hatred, exclusion, and unkindness that exist outside their doors. I identify as a member of the Black British diaspora. I have one child, also black, aged 22, who is short and slight in body and often wears a hoodie. When my child steps outside the door, I pray, as do most parents, that they will make it home. Two weeks ago, this is what happened to my child on the way home from work, around 11.30 at night. The bus driver, after letting five passengers off, refused to let my child on. 'We are full', he said. So my child started to walk home in the dark. As they walked home, on a main Birmingham road, a car slowed, the window was lowered, and two water balloons flew out, hitting my child, and the driver and passengers drove away, laughing. My prayers were answered: my child made it home – but soaking wet, traumatised, and in emotional distress.

In his book, *Is God Colour Blind?*, Professor Anthony Reddie, a lecturer at Oxford University, writes:

> Racism, sexism, patriarchy, homophobia, ageism, classism, among
> other things, all intrinsically deny the love of God because their
> perpetrators fail to love the wisdom of God that has given them
> relational opportunities to love their neighbour, often when that
> neighbour is not like them.[1]

Friends, we have listened to some wonderful speakers this week. They have given us a broad outlook on relational opportunities, right relationship, sometimes reflecting on the issues raised by Anthony Reddie. Each of the -isms listed in the quotation from his book relates to our individual identities. Some identities are hidden, some are not. Although all of these identities can be said to encounter prejudice, hate, and discrimination in many forms, including micro-aggressions, systemic denial, and violence, and although these -isms often intersect with the multiplicity of our identities, Cody and I invite you to focus with us on the arena of right relationship with racism, and right relationship with repair, as people who are challenged to love their neighbour who may appear *not* like them. This conversation may become a little uncomfortable, but bear with us. Give yourself permission to sit with the dis-ease, the discomfort. So, take a deep breath as we traverse a minefield of emotions. ...

... On 25 May 2020 the world was shaken by an inhumane act that resulted in the murder of a man called George Floyd, in Minnesota, by several police officers, but mainly Officer Derek Chauvin as he knelt on George's neck and back, restricting his breathing. I said the world was *shaken* rather than *shocked* because millions of black people and people of colour were not shocked. It was not the first time that an innocent black person was killed by a public servant employed to protect them. And it would not be the last time. And, lest you feel that this is solely an American problem, let me invite you to do the research yourself, or

---

[1]   Anthony G. Reddie, *Is God Colour Blind? Insights from Black Theology for Christian Faith and Ministry* (Society for Promoting Christian Knowledge, London, 2nd. ed., 2020, p. 33).

read the report written by Ian Minter, a member of the Birmingham Unitarian community, who spent two years researching 'black and blue' deaths (deaths of black people at the hands of police officers or prison officers) in the UK and found, over a 40-year period, three dozen fatalities caused by asphyxiation and positional restraint: the same cause that killed George Floyd.

I digress. But what George Floyd's death did for the world was to highlight the inequity that black and brown bodies in white-majority countries experience. There were riots, marches, and protests all over the world. Conversations took place. More people came out and spoke about their lived experience of racism, and people *listened*. Such beautiful formations of right relationship happened in the aftermath of George's death. Words describing racist behaviour, not new, but known only by few, were introduced. I myself learned new words and phrases which accurately described the experiences that I myself had encountered for most of my life: *tone policing, white apathy, white privilege, anti-blackness, white silence, micro-invalidation, micro-assault, micro-insult, gaslighting, white racial conditioning.* Jane Blackall spoke the truth in her talk at the start of this Summer School: 'Just because it's normal doesn't mean it's right'.

I was used to the ugliness of racism, of overt name calling and being told to go back to my jungle. Or being hit at in the street, or intimidated in a bar because I was a 'black b***'. I was used to the monkey chants, the banana references, and 'big mama' jokes. But what I lacked was the language to articulate the subtle, indirect, smiley racism that gave me the stone-in-the-pit-of-my-stomach feeling. That kind of racism, with its subliminal messaging, is hard to prove. But it produced experiences that did not sit right with me, that forced me into a relationship of masking, hypervigilance, and fear, where I was left afraid to speak my truth.

Eduardo Bonilla-Silva, Professor of Sociology at Duke University in North Carolina, tells us in his book *Racism without Racists* that we are living in a new ideology of racism, called 'colour-blind racism'. It is a racism that is more subtle than simple name-calling or the burning of crosses by men dressed in white sheets. A racism that is covert, systemic, and institutionalised. A racism steeped in criticism of 'the other', their values, morality, and work ethics ... and a racism that proclaims white people to be victims of supposedly 'reverse racism'.[2] His words express our current situation. Be it England, Wales, Scotland, or Ireland. Be it the United States or Canada, Australia or France, we live today in a world where many proclaim that they are *not racist* … and yet racism is occurring. Please believe me when I say that I rarely call anyone racist who does not self-identify as such. (Certain politicians are the exception.)

I do believe that we live in a world embedded with racist ideas, a world that implicitly and explicitly has voiced racial stereotypes, and entrenched racism in our policies and institutions. And because of our upbringing, our schooling, the history we learned, the books we were forced to read, the artworks in our museums, and the fears of 'the other' that our loved ones have imbued in us, we have all absorbed racialised ideologies, and can easily spew out racist ideas and expressions without any intention of being racist.

May I draw your attention to the definition proposed by Ibram X Kendi, a writer, professor, anti-racism activist, and historian. He was also the Ware Lecture Speaker (similar to our John Relly Beard Keynote Speaker) at the Unitarian Universalist 2022 General Assembly annual conference. He offers the following definitions:

> A racist (person): one who is supporting a racist policy through their actions or inaction, or expressing a racist idea.
> Antiracist (person): one who is supporting an antiracist policy through their actions, or expressing an antiracist idea.[3]

I like Kendi's definitions, because they explain how we can easily spew racist ideology even without intending to do so. Moreover, he explains how we can evolve into being the opposite, an anti-racist, through our actions.

---

2   Eduardo Bonilla-Silva, *Racism Without Racists: Color-Blind Racism and the Persistence of Racial Inequality in the United States* (Rowman & Littlefield, 2003, pp. 3–4).

3   Ibram X. Kendi, *How To Be An Antiracist* (Penguin/Vintage, London, 2019, p. 13).

But note that there is no 'not racist'. You can only be racist or anti-racist, and you can't be anti-racist by doing nothing. Anti-racism is not possible through inaction. One must be actioning or expressing anti-racist ideas. I also like Kendi's definition because it is defined by the impact, not the intention, of an action. You may not intend to support racist policies, ideas, practices, traditions, but unless you actively support ANTI-Racism, it is your impact that defines your label. It's a bit like, 'You may intend not to be pregnant, but the impact is that you are.'

The danger lies in not knowing that something is racist. Not accepting the lived experience of the other when they say that your words or action have done harm. The denial. The danger lies in doing nothing, in changing nothing. You are the fear that is perpetuating racism.

As faith people, we understand mistakes. But as faith people we must also lean into learning from our mistakes, so that we can build right relationships. We must be on guard for the colour-blind mentality that refuses to acknowledge historical legacies and racialised structures, insisting that racism is individual. We must be on guard against the common generalisation of People of Colour as a homogeneous stereotypical group: as young thugs, or single-parent benefit takers with absentee fathers, etc. We People of Colour must be on guard, for we have not reached the promised land foreseen by Dr Martin Luther King Junior, where in a white-majority nation we will not be judged by the colour of our skin but by the content of our character. We must be on our guard.

'I don't see colour.'
'They aren't black! They are just people.'
'We didn't have slaves here.'
'They just need to get over it. The past is the past.'
'I treat all people the same, regardless of colour.'
'I didn't get the job, because they gave it to a black man.'
'Talking about different races is divisive.'

Do these phrases sound familiar to you? They are to me. All are examples of colour-blind racism that have been heard in our white-majority UK Unitarian churches.

As I navigate the systems and structures that lay down the rules of civility in school, in church, at work, in friendships, I engage in the apparatus of state-sponsored systemic manipulation. Systems of minimisation that mould what I am allowed to know, allowed to do, allowed to say, allowed to wear, and who I am allowed to be. It is a relationship of fear. Fear of getting things wrong, fear of saying things to contradict others, even while telling the truth of the situation. Fear that I will be labelled, politicised, ostracised, in ways that make me hated and harmed. And often, as the only non-white person in whiteness spaces, I am left with the option of not speaking up, and therefore perpetuating the status quo. Not offering up the other perspective, often unwelcomed, often uncomfortable to the ears hearing it.

If you are one that does not see race, then how can you profess to want to be in right relationship with me? I see my African-Caribbean heritage in the darkness of my black skin, and I celebrate it. What do you see? If you never see race, then you never see the racism experienced each day by millions of People of Colour. Do you ever see the young black men stopped and searched by police officers and ask yourself why *you* weren't stopped? Or do you, like the priest and the Levite in the story of the good Samaritan in Luke's Gospel, walk on by?

How often do you see the security guard when you enter a shop? Once? Twice? On entry and exit? Or do you see them out of the corner of your eye as you journey down different aisles? As you pick something up? By the cash register? And are you stopped at the door to prove your purchases because your items are not in a bag? Those are the experiences of some People of Colour. It is why Black parents train their kids always to get a receipt.

When the question of slavery is brought up and your considered answer is *'We didn't have slavery here'*, were you even considering all those enslaved black and brown people who were brought to England as slaves, given as gifts, or sold at auction houses in London and made to live as slaves while they were here? Or the 800,000 British-owned enslaved people supposedly freed at the abolition of slavery in 1833, but made to continue their servitude, under the guise of apprenticeship, for another four years, despite being called *freed*. Or the compensation of

£20 million (£16 *billion* in today's money) paid to British slave owners, while the 800,000 freed slaves received nothing.

Now consider the fact that the descendants of those enslaved people, paying taxes between 1833 and 2015, paid back the money given by the government to those slaveowners. Consider those black and brown men and women in this country today who have paid for those slaveowners' compensation through their taxes, and tell me that slavery is the past. Tell me you don't feel sick at the injustice, the inequality of it all. Sarah and Jane were right when they started the week telling us that right relationship is tricky, especially when we have a national history of not recognising the spark of divinity in *all* people. Change has taken time, and speaking truth is difficult to hear, as well as to do.

When you don't see how all this affects my race, impacts my life as a person of colour and a mother, messes with my psyche with each killing as I worry if my child will get home tonight. When you don't see each stop and search, each arrest, each battery of black and brown bodies, and ponder the intersection of race in these actions. When you cannot have meaningful discussions on racism, and fail to reflect on your privileges and fragility, how can we move into right relationship with each other?

Let's think for a moment on this while we listen to some music: Paul McCartney singing *Blackbird*.[4] He wrote *Blackbird* in the 1960s as he watched black people in America gain their civil rights. The blackbird is a black woman finally getting freedom to vote and sit at the front of the bus. Yet freedom from racism has yet to be achieved.

I am going to be honest and say that right relationship with racial equity requires a move into reparation. Reparation defined as 'the action of making amends for a wrong one has done, by providing payment or other assistance to those who have been wronged'.[5] To make amends is to repair the relationship by recognising the inherent worth and dignity of *the othered*. To make whole again what was broken generations ago by injustice that is still perpetuated today.

---

4   https://youtu.be/JiL5JpUtjqY
5   From Google's English Dictionary, provided by Oxford Languages.

Right relationship is the appreciation and compassion for one another expressed by the Samaritan who STOPPED, who, to quote 'Love Beyond God', a poem by Adam Lawrence Dyer,[6] 'tasted the tears' of the other and loved beyond their fear, and it was GOOD. Lizzie Kingston-Harrison and Nicola Temple reminded us in their talk to note who is not in the room, who is not around the table: the one that we are not in right relationship with.

Repair, REPARATION, means taking responsibility and accountability for the wrong done, and doing that in numerous ways, including through education, violence prevention, and understanding decolonisation, in order to be proactive in creating an anti-racist environment at home, in schools, at work, in our health-care and prison systems, in our policing, the law, the environment, immigration, agriculture, food, housing, and churches. That way anti-racism becomes the norm in all our social systems and structures.

Jill Strauss, co-editor of the book *Slavery's Descendants: Shared Legacies of Race and Reconciliation*,[7] and teacher of Conflict Resolution and Communications at Manhattan Community College New York, asks, 'How do we make right in the present what our ancestors did to other people?' In reality, no one present today can override the past and make right the wrong that was done. But what we can do is work at creating, cultivating, and maintaining right relationship with each other in the present, and in the future.

In an article entitled 'Now You See Me, Now You Don't', Professor Anthony Reddie argues: 'White invisibility and normality remain a crucial socio-cultural and political signifier in the construction of Britishness and Englishness within the Body politic of the nation', where claims that 'we have always done it this way', and 'we don't see colour', perpetuate a culture of assimilation and a fear-based relationship of not wanting to rock the boat.[8]

---

6   Adam Lawrence Dyer, *Love Beyond God: Meditations* (Skinner House Books, Boston, 2016).

7   Rutgers University Press, 2019.

8   Anthony G. Reddie (2018) 'Now you see me, now you don't: subjectivity, blackness, and difference in practical theology in Britain post Brexit', *Practical Theology*, 11:1, 4–16.

'*You're from Africa, right, Winnie*', a teacher once said, pointing to my brown skin when presenting a session on slavery in a history lesson.

'*No, Miss, I'm a Brummie*', I replied.

'*That's not what I mean, and you know it*', the teacher said in a stern voice, looking down at me crossly. '*We don't have people with your skin here. You all come from Africa, like the slaves.*'

The class sniggered. I was annoyed. Why did she pick on me? Why did our first (and only) lesson about black people in history have to be on slavery? Why not Marcus Garvey, Malcolm X, or Queen Nefertiti?

'*I was born in Birmingham, Miss, not Africa. And my parents are from Jamaica.*'

In remembering this incident of micro-invalidation (implying that I don't belong, that my citizenship is not British) at my secondary school, I remember too what happened in the playground that afternoon. The name-calling, the references to apes, being told to return to the jungle, the feeling of being *less than*. I hated history lessons after that. I didn't do History for GCSE. I felt othered. I recognise now that, as a teenager, I rocked the boat. But not often, as I attempted to 'fit in', assimilate into British whiteness culture. I fear that sometimes I did it too well, as I experienced more than once, standing in a group of white friends who were complaining about black people, using racial slurs. Suddenly they would remember that I was black, and they would say, "*Not you, Winnie, I don't mean you ... you're not like the others.*' Now, imagine the hostility directed towards my brown sisters wearing the hijab or burka when people make assumptions about their reason for wearing it. Is it really a sign of oppression, or is it a source of dignity and connection with their cultural heritage, and family? Gordon Willard Allport, psychologist, in his book *The Nature of Prejudice*,[9] tells us: 'we prize our own mode of existence and correspondingly underprize or actively attack what seems to us to threaten it'.

The socio-cultural construct of whiteness in these British lands is present in many structures of our society: in education, work, politics,

9   Addison-Wesley, 1954.

health care, and churches. And as Unitarians we are called to rise and break out of our fear and suspicion, work on our implicit biases (including me) and our structures that maintain racism, and journey into right relationship. This is big work. Arek Malecki and Laura Dobson have spoken to us about how we can be in right relationship with our body, engaging with who we are in a physical sense. People of colour need space to do that in our worship too: to feel invited in, to praise with our bodies in movement, in meditation, in dance, in ritual. The impact could be powerful and revolutionary, cultivating spaces of faith, and, as Arek and Laura expressed it, paying attention to our chest as it expands with breath, gratitude, joy, love, and even sorrow.

You and I, black, white, brown, or mixed-heritage, are harmed by white-supremacy culture as it affects all of us; as it prevents us from engaging in interconnectedness and right relationships. But we are not defined by this whiteness culture. It informs us and our structures, but it can be deconstructed and replaced. Faith challenges us to commit ourselves to racial equity in more than intention: in action and expression.

It won't be an easy relationship, as society perceives diversity and '*wokeness*' as dirty words. Conversations on race are difficult, but we must not close them down by manoeuvring the conversation away from the subject, nor by focusing on class instead of race, nor equating racism to other -isms such as gender inequality, classism, or homophobia. All these equally deserve conversations, but we need a time to focus also on race and place it at the centre of our conversations – otherwise the systemic structure of racial inequality will remain the status quo.

As Unitarians we need to recognise our own status as a predominantly white, whiteness-centred denomination. We have to acknowledge the privileges that exist within this denomination, including privileges influencing the way we do worship, centred on a whiteness culture of liturgy, of readings rather than moved-by-the-spirit spontaneity, of hymns with 19th-century tunes and metres, of readings of texts written by predominantly white authors (with a few Sufi poems thrown in). Contributions from other cultures must not be relegated to slots such as Black History Month or LGBT Month. And, as Alex Brianson and Tor Glinwell urged us yesterday, hidden disabilities and genders, sexuality and neurodiversity also need to be acknowledged and included in the way we do worship if we want to cultivate a space of right relationship. We have to acknowledge that in this day and age a whiteness-centred, heterosexual normativity is not OK, and it is not inclusive or welcoming.

Also, we need to repair the instruction to be silent or to silence others in the face of racist remarks, or jokes. Repair the instruction to dress quietly in sober colours and adopt acceptable hair styles. Repair the implicit requirement – the tone policing – to be still, to swallow your amen or your hallelujah or claps. A healing is called for, and reparation in the form of over-compensated listening, over-compensated learning, over-compensated defending the Other is needed.

Unitarians need to right the relationships that wronged others – relationships formed and perpetuated by their ancestors, their teachers, their loved ones, their politicians – by engaging in anti-oppression, anti-white-supremacy education, decolonisation, and healing the pains of exclusion. When diversity is involved and valued, differences are bridged, and all parts of our relationship with each other are restored, then we will have recognised the inherent worth and dignity of every person, and we will love our neighbours as ourselves.

May we do so.

Questions for Reflection and Discussion

1. What micro-aggressions are you familiar with? How are they harmful to People of Colour in particular?

2. What actions and expressions can we engage in to disrupt 'whiteness' in our congregations, in order to facilitate right relationships?

3. In order to engage in discussions about the repair of relationships, can you name and explore the actions of individuals in your congregation's history who were (a) slaveowners or (b) abolitionists?

4. If you call yourself 'not racist', what anti-racist policies do you support, and what anti-racist actions have you undertaken?

The author

Revd Winnie Gordon identifies as a member of the Black British Diaspora with a multiplicity of heritages: queer, mother, Minister in the Unitarian faith serving the Birmingham New Meeting congregation, and Tutor/Assessor at Unitarian College. 'I am a product of colonialism through heritage, and post-colonialism through birth.' Divorced from the Christian faith of her birth, Winnie found Unitarianism in 2006 and qualified as a Minister in 2013. She has been a theme speaker and co-facilitator at several Summer Schools, and has had a long involvement with the Worship Studies Course. More recently, Winnie completed a Master of Research Degree investigating the inclusivity of People of Colour in UK Unitarian worship communities. She is involved with a local Birmingham charity, Ladywood Community Project, which supports families experiencing financial hardship.

6 Right Relationship: Repair as a Sacred Task

Cody Coyne

It is hard to talk about 'Repair' without falling into a thicket of questions: what needs repairing? Why do we think it is broken? Whose fault is it? If it is restored, will it be 'as good as new'? These questions arise whether the object in need of repair is something mundane, like a toaster, or something monumental, like an aeroplane. And when we reflect on 'Repair' in the context of human life, the questions gain a deeper significance and urgency: How do we create right relationship? How do we create it when we are wounded by others – and when we ourselves cause pain?

We should not expect life to answer these questions easily. We may never fully achieve Right Relationship, at least by any appreciable measure. 'We are always fumbling around', to quote Sarah Tinker's theme talk. Much religious literature is geared towards accepting the existence of pain, whether it is Buddha's dictum 'All is Dukkha [suffering]', or Jesus' question 'Does not the rain fall on the just and unjust?', or Hinduism's Wheel of Samsara. The Serenity Prayer reminds us to 'accept the things we cannot change' – which for many people is an acknowledgement that the world that we wish for is rarely the world that we see. Injury and wounded-ness are part of life. Kahlil Gibran, in his poetic work *The Prophet*, finds pain even in the embrace of love:

> *When [love's] wings enfold you, yield to him,*
> *though the sword hidden among his pinions may wound you.*[1]

---

1   Kahlil Gibran, *The Prophet* (Alfred A. Knopf, New York, 1923).

Gibran continues with an analogy about pruning and growth: a gardener's image familiar to many. He teaches that experiencing pain, suffering discomfort, is part of our growth; that we become better people – more compassionate, or stronger. 'No pain, no gain', we are often glibly told. And perhaps this is the case, some of the time. But consider: how convenient is this proposition for those who do the wounding? In a culture where, when people are held to account, they claim that they are being 'cancelled', where hurtful words are shared by people gleefully proclaiming them to be 'politically incorrect', where reasoned arguments are met with the taunt 'Grow up, snowflake!', the image of painful growth is embedded so deep in Western culture as to calcify and harden the hearts of its adherents. This is truly a time to be counter-cultural. Are there times when the injury is too great to repair? What is 'right relationship' when someone feels belittled by another person in their church or chapel? How far can our tolerance bend? And how far should we bend? Under what circumstances is relationship severed? And when it is, is there any way for it to be a 'right un-relationship'?

I am getting ahead of myself. We are considering 'Repair' in Right Relationship. Recently I have reflected on people who have been in my life for a while, particularly those in the church, who have stayed or left, or left and subsequently returned. When I began my ministry, I felt that a large blockage preventing denominational growth was our own dysfunction. Micro-aggressions, passive aggressions, back-stabbing, providing selective information, using the expression 'People are saying ...': these behaviours can create an atmosphere that is harmful to growth. A community can carry on despite these behaviours, for sure; but it will not be seen as a loving community.

What is more, these habits are far more evident to people outside a chapel than to those inside. We become inured to them, unaware that they are occurring, or we justify them with comments such as 'Well, that's just what so-and-so does'. But to someone coming to us from the outside, a church complicit in such behaviours will quickly lose its lustre of Sacred Care and Compassion. People who walk through the doors and hear belittling comments, or witness sabotage and animus, will understand that the church and its members are not in

'Right Relationship' with each other. Which may feel unfair, as we have accepted that mistakes and injury are part of life. We should be given some measure of tolerance, some opportunity to re-establish Loving Bonds, some gift of grace or forgiveness. We want a recognition of our humanness, and we hope that the visitor will grant us that much.

And if Right Relationship honours the individuals concerned, it will honour their humanness, including their capacity to err. For me, Right Relationship seeks to grant people the fullness of their being in connection with Others. And when this fullness is not honoured, or the connection is strained, we need to repair the relationship. It is a process that includes acceptance of error and humanness, vulnerability and trust, and corrective action.

Within the ancient Hebrew tradition, sacred bonds were described as Covenants. In Jewish scripture, Yahweh made Covenants with Adam, Noah, Abraham, and Moses. In the New Testament, Jesus speaks of Covenant with the pouring of wine: 'This is my blood of the covenant, which is poured out for many for the forgiveness of sin'. Covenants, as bonds, provide opportunities for reconciliation and repair. They are not simply contracts that can be torn up, but instead they offer mechanisms – rituals, reparations, recognition – to care for the relationship and draw together that which has been torn apart. So several years ago my own congregation adopted a covenant. People were asked to reflect on how they would want to be treated; on the reasons why they came to church; and how they wanted the church to be seen and understood by others. And, with a bit of give-and-take, we settled on the following:

We are gathered here in sacred fellowship
To witness the fullness of our lives and all life,
To hold and be held, tell stories and listen,
To be renewed and renew the world.
We speak with care and patience,
We act with gentleness and compassion,
We forgive each other and ourselves.
In faith that we build beloved community,
We renew our covenant today.

This weekly affirmation was to help the congregation feel bound together with a regular commitment. Historically Christian churches are rooted in a re-commitment after errancy: a week's worth of mistakes is sufficient to take into the church and be absolved. Although our Unitarian theology may be different, many people still approach our church with a sense of re-affirming their goodness, despite any mis-steps that they may take from Monday to Saturday. Although we are not bound by a theological creed, I felt that our covenant was open enough for most people to feel comfortable saying it. That was the primary reason.

The secondary reason was to produce a statement that could be cited when boundaries were overstepped. Not in a binding way, or a formal way, but as a touchstone that we might grasp when engaging with difficult behaviour. Covenants refer more to action than to belief, and so our congregation was making a commitment to act more lovingly. When necessary, we could refer to this call to speak with care and act with gentleness, and draw people back into Right Relationship.

That was my theory, but it has played out differently in practice. I might reflect on it before a challenging conversation is due to take place, or if I feel that I have been called to account. However, when Repair is necessary in a church, the environment is charged: tensions run high, emotions overflow, defences are at the ready. People feel their vulnerability and push against it, often unconsciously, sometimes following a familiar pattern.

Elizabeth Kübler-Ross wrote of the five stages of grief,[2] observing that when someone needs to be held to account, they will be grieving. It may be that they are grieving for the injury that they have caused. They may be grieving for the possibility of losing a relationship. They may be grieving for their own injured ego. This is not to deny the pain that they have caused, or the boundaries that they have overstepped. But we are talking about right 'relationship', and so, when someone affronts another, they themselves suffer as well.

---

2   Elizabeth Kübler-Ross, *On Death and Dying* (The Macmillan Company, New York, 1969).

Kübler-Ross names the first stage of grief as **Denial**. We should acknowledge that people go through the stages in different ways, or return to various stages at different times. But I have so often seen the first response in a conversation about hurtful behaviour to be some form of denial. It may not be a complete denial of events (although I have seen that); but it will very likely be some form of justification. It's not denying the action, but denying the harm that it has caused. I have seen offensive language justified. I have seen aggressive behaviour justified. I have seen destruction of church property justified. And to ensure that this talk is not one-sided, I have seen myself justify acts that were clearly painful for others. So I can speak of how, in that heat of the moment, when faced with the reality of the consequences of our actions, the path of justification and denial is perceived to be the easier route.

The second stage of grief, using Kübler-Ross's model, is **Anger**. When the severity of the action becomes apparent or undeniable, the accused may become belligerent. I have been openly called a lot of things (which makes me curious to know what has been said behind my back) when people have been called to account. And again, for balance, in the heat of the moment I have found myself using a rising voice, sharper and louder, and regrettable words: responses intended to resist the truth of the grief that I have caused.

We may find examples of other stages of grief in our arsenal: **Bargaining** ('I would not mind what I did if you did it to me'), and **Despondency** ('My behaviour has proven me to be beyond redemption'). The final stage, of course, is **Acceptance**, when one finally submits to becoming vulnerable in the process, very often with an apology. Repairing Right Relationship requires vulnerability.

It could be argued that these stages, when dealing with hurtful behaviour, are defence tactics of the ego. That may be the case. But we can grieve for our participation in a hurt-filled world, and that grief may take time and processing before it can be acknowledged fully.

Other means of Repair are possible: when a covenant is broken, one method of resolution is called 'Ouch / oops'. The idea is that if someone oversteps a boundary – saying something hurtful, for instance – the person who has been hurt has an opportunity to say 'Ouch' – to explain why the words were hurtful, or assumptive, or otherwise. The person who committed the injustice then has an opportunity to say 'Oops': to own their action, and recommit to the relationship. The levity of the expression 'Ouch / oops' can help tense situations to cool down a bit.

Witnessing the use of these resolution techniques opened my eyes to the challenge of dysfunction, which I felt was the major problem facing us in our church. Root out dysfunction, and we would experience a greater level of growth. But although I could feel confident that many forms of dysfunction were being addressed, I saw that new forms of dysfunction often replaced the old. I became aware that one could not simply revamp the system overnight; not only was this going to be a long haul, it was a garden that required constant upkeep. For a relationship to be vibrant, it has to be responsive: living, shifting, growing as the participants grow. And this applies not just to two people, but to larger groups: the relationship between congregant and church, or the Church and the wider community. These relationships require a living commitment, continuously listening to the needs and opportunities of people often deemed 'Different'. Making amends and changing, to support even more of Creation's diversity. When done well, Repair not only restores Right Relationship but actually strengthens it. Over-stepping boundaries at times, but with the expectancy that this will happen, and with the willingness to grow and change, helps to foster trust. And with a greater sense of trust, we can engage in our relationships more authentically, more fully, knowing that our mistakes will not sever the bonds that we have formed. Acknowledgement, apology, and corrective action are necessary for the preservation of a relationship.

But only to a degree. I said that Repair is healthy and good, when done well. But it is not always done well. People get stuck in those cycles of denial and anger. Sometimes the action leaves such deep marks that healing will take a lifetime. Sometimes one risks one's own safety by perpetuating a relationship. And sometimes the core of a relationship is unhealthy. To examine Right Relationship requires acknowledging Broken Relationships, or, as I said earlier, 'Right un-Relationship'.

But how do we achieve a 'Right un-Relationship'? Like Repair, it is hard to gauge, because we rarely see it in our culture. When people do attempt it, society can be cynical at best, and mocking at worst. More than a decade ago, Gwyneth Paltrow and her husband Chris Martin announced that they were undergoing a 'Conscious Uncoupling': an expression which prompted mirth and derision in the media. Closer to home, a good friend of mine describes the bemusement that she faces when telling people how close she is to her ex-wife. However, I have begun to realise that those individuals were still in 'Right Relationship'. My friend and her ex-wife continue to bolster and enlarge the other's life; does the fact of their legal divorce negate the spiritual care that they provide for one another? I realised that it was my own cultural baggage that caused me to imagine them as an 'un-Relationship'. But the fact that their love is manifested differently from before – that it has evolved in response to new circumstances – demonstrates that Repair is possible.

The reasons that prompt people to separate often mean that the break cannot be done cleanly, or amicably, or mutually. A Relationship incapable of Repair is likely to be seen differently by the different parties, advantageous to one and disadvantageous to the other. Even when the reality of these discrepancies is known, a way to reconnect may not feel possible. It is like a bridge built from two sides, without proper planning for how to meet in the middle. Time may assist the process, as well as reflection, and (if your theology works in this way) prayer. Individuals who cause injury to another are often themselves injured; understanding the cycles that people that get caught up in may help those who have been injured in relationships. Several years ago my Cross Street Chapel hosted an exhibition called 'The Forgiveness Project'. It featured a number of stories about people who had suffered dearly, or who had caused injury, and their subsequent journeys to forgiveness. The exhibition concluded with a talk by Figen Murray, whose son Martyn Hett was killed in the Manchester Arena Bombing in 2017. Figen, in addition to her efforts to persuade Parliament to pass a law to strengthen security measures at large venues, emerged as a victim who was prepared to forgive the man who killed her son.

Forgiveness can serve both as a means of Repair, and as a way to create 'Right un-Relationship'. It may be used to help restore bonds that had broken long ago, and it can also serve as a way for an individual to reaffirm their disconnect from a harmful relationship. Speaking of her experience, Figen draws on the outpouring of love that her son Martyn shared with the world. Her act of forgiveness has allowed her to process some of the pain and to carry on, recommitted to building a safer and more loving world. But her story is not everyone's story. And we would be committing a grave injustice to expect all victims to forgive as she has. Forgiveness is a powerful tool. Some victims can move on only when they have used it. Others hold it in preparation for Repair. Even 'The Forgiveness Project' included a story that had not been resolved through Forgiveness.

Repair plays a significant part in maintaining right relationship. It involves understanding the boundaries of our being and wellness, and respecting those boundaries set by other people. Right relationship necessarily involves error and repair. However, sometimes relationship cannot be right, or repaired, and so we need to prepare for times when bonds must be broken.

Repair is not easy: it is often a messy process, and it can take a long time. It may require compromise, listening, and forgiveness: all skills that rarely receive headline space in today's world. But to maintain Right Relationship, to exist in community with others while maintaining our full humanity, is a Divine Blessing worthy of such work.

Questions for Reflection and Discussion

1. Recall a period in your life when a close relationship felt strained, but eventually found resolution. What led to the resolution? How did the people involved navigate different emotions and achieve empathy?

2. What can our churches do to become better stewards of right relationship, especially in terms of repairing relationships?

3. What role does the church have in repairing social relationships? Can the church serve as a mediating voice between parties? Does it have its own repair to conduct?

4. Have you ever had to say goodbye to a relationship? What helped the process at the time? What might you have done differently?

The author

Revd Cody Coyne was born in Flint, Michigan, where he attended the local Unitarian-Universalist church with his family. He began his ministerial training at Harris Manchester College, Oxford, in 2011. In 2015 he was appointed minister at Cross Street Unitarian Chapel in Manchester. In addition to his ministry, he serves on the executive of the Manchester Unitarian District Association and the Unitarian Peace Fellowship. He is also a trustee of the Faith Network for Manchester, a charity dedicated to interfaith dialogue and co-operation. He is also a participant in Manchester's 'Challenging Hate Forum', an inter-faith and inter-civic group working to combat hate crime, and he has assisted Manchester's interfaith celebration 'Peace and Unity'.

PART TWO

Real Life: Telling the Truth of our Lived Experience

(Summer School 2023)

Louise Baumberg

7 Introduction

The theme of the 2023 Summer School is 'Real Life: Telling the Truth of our Lived Experience'. So, here I am, a real person with my own lived experience, just as we all are real, with our own unique lived experiences. I hope that my contributions will provide food for thought for you all – and a jumping-off point for your ideas too. I will warn you: I don't have all the answers. I don't even have all the questions!

I first attended Summer School more than 10 years ago. When I was thinking of coming, my minister at the time remarked: 'It's very intense', and I don't necessarily think she meant that in a good way; maybe she was trying to manage my expectations. Fortunately I still came, with my two children, and had a great time. Yes, it was quite intense, but as a mother of two, working part time, the fact that all the chores of shopping, cooking, clearing up, and entertaining children were taken care of meant that I had time to listen, reflect, and talk more than I ever could at home.

Perhaps including banal considerations such as household chores in a Theme Talk is somehow inappropriate – not 'spiritual' enough. But surely this is what is encompassed in our theme? Household chores, everyday niggles and joys, stain removal and accessible toilets (to name just a few issues important to people who have periods, or are messy eaters, or cricket parents, or unable to access regular toilets) *are* real life. They are the truth of our lived experiences.

At that first Summer School I found a community of overwhelmingly kind people, thoughtful people, good listeners. It was a place where it felt safe to share, and a place where I felt accepted. And I hope that you are as excited as I am to be back here at Summer School, four years since our last in-person event. And if this is your first time, I hope you are not too apprehensive. A lot has happened over the last four years, much of it hugely difficult. It may be painful to think about that time, or you may feel that it needs to be spoken about because we are in danger of forgetting. People all over the world, and here in this room, will have experienced illness, bereavement, poverty, loneliness, mental-health challenges, and other dark times which may be continuing to affect life today. Speaking my own truth very briefly, I must say that the onset of Covid-19 in March 2020 resulted in some horribly stressful family issues, some of which have had long-term effects on myself and others close to me. It can be very hard to speak those truths and hear those truths. And yet others had different experiences. An acquaintance of mine had 'a lovely family time' during the lockdowns. That was her truth, but boy was it hard for me to hear!

During the coming week I will be speaking about the stories that we tell about our lives, our place in the world, and its impact on our stories, and how our experiences and the people that we are can be invisible, misunderstood, marginalised, or vilified. Then I will look at how we can make space for all of our stories to be heard, in an ideal world but also in the flawed reality in which we live.

You might say to me: who are you as a white, cisgender, heterosexual, neurotypical, healthy, middle-class woman, who has never known financial hardship and has secure citizenship, to speak about those who are different, invisible, unheard? It's a good question, and one for which I have only a partial answer. As you hear what I say, I hope that it will spark or resonate with your own thoughts, your own interpretations, and that you will think of your own stories. The way that we relate to each other in our engagement groups will, I hope, be an exemplar of an attitude and a space where we can be real, where we can each tell the truth of our lived experience and feel safe and heard. We have a chance this week to live in community and relate to each other – truly listening and feeling safe to share our truths. And so the Theme Talks are just one part of what we will be creating together. Summer School always was a special community, if only for a week, so now we are back in person we will continue that tradition. I believe that we can take it further: we can try to be intentional, deliberate, in the way that we relate to each other in this precious space that we have. And each and every one of us has something to contribute.

It sometimes seems that the world is getting harsher – more combative, more polarised, with less respect between people. I can't say for sure, because in some contexts great improvements are taking place. And the bad things always get more exposure, because of the shock value that drives clicks and advertising. But I do know that there is lots of scary stuff out there, and places where we can't feel safe to share the truth of our lived experience. We see people being torn down, and we can't help them. We might be fearful of 'being real' in case of hostile comments, either in person or online. And not just hostile comments: out there in the real world there are places where to be LGBTQ+ and be your authentic self means that your life is threatened. There are places and situations where to be a person of colour means an additional, unfair risk of harm when just going about the business of everyday living.

So we try, here, whether in person or online, to make a different world, just for a week. To show that the effort is worthwhile. We know that we are in a privileged space, with our meals provided and few domestic stresses (yes, I'm talking about cooking and washing up again). We have of course brought ourselves, our whole selves, and with us we have brought stresses: anxieties for the future, difficulties of the present, regrets from the past. We have brought our own prejudices with us, our insecurities, our sadnesses.

You may have heard of Martin Buber, the Jewish philosopher, existentialist, and nominee for the Nobel Literature and Peace prizes. His writings on dialogue and relationships between people were particularly influential. He writes (and I have changed his language so that it speaks to us more universally):

> The basis of human life is twofold, and it is the wish of every
> person to be confirmed as what they are, even as what they can
> become, by other people: and the innate capacity in humankind to
> confirm their fellow humans in this way ... Actual humanity exists
> only where this capacity unfolds.[1]

---

1   M. Buber, 'Distance and Relation', *Hibbert Journal: Quarterly Review of Religion, Theology and Philosophy* Vol. XLIX (2), pp. 105–114 (1951).

This is the basis of respect, the basis of justice, the basis of peace, and we would love this to be the basis of Summer School as well. Let us confirm our fellow humans as what they are and what they can become, and let us be so confirmed. Are you with me?

Question for Reflection and Discussion

How do you feel about 'being real' with others?

---

8 Stories of Our Lives

Today on our journey of considering 'Real life – the truth of our lived experience', I want to look at stories. True stories, obviously, but still stories. How we tell them, what we might be leaving out, and the truly life-changing benefits that we see from telling them and being heard.

Our lives, and indeed our identities, are a product of all of our lived experiences. But where to start? What to include? Looking at my own life, I could tell you about my family. But it would take too long to include that whole story from childhood to the present. I could speak about my education and my work history, about my ups and downs in mental health; I could tell you about the geography of my life – places that I have lived in and travelled to. There are my hobbies, my spiritual journey, my friendships, and so on. Or just snippets: the pleasure that I get from hanging washing outside to dry, the frustration I feel when my foster-son picks his eczema, the anger and despair I feel about political decisions and ineptitude that cause so much suffering in this country and around the world. Not to mention the struggle to maintain emotional equilibrium while living with three teenage boys!

Much of my work and family life since 2016/17 has involved refugees. We became foster carers in 2017, in response to the refugee crisis of 2016, and we have been welcoming unaccompanied asylum-seeking children into the family since then. Our youngest son, now adopted, came to us first as an unaccompanied asylum seeker more than four years ago. In 2018 I began studying for an MA in Refugee Care. I learned a lot that was useful and relevant for working with refugees, but much also that contributed a really useful perspective on any human interactions, circumstances, or systems. So please bear in mind that when I offer examples from the refugee experience, these can apply to virtually any human interactions, or situations.

* * * * * *

Let me tell you a true story that happened in a far-away place, but not long ago. Christmas Island is an Australian territory, a small tropical island south of Java, about 2,000 km from the Australian mainland. It is one of the islands on which Australia has installed an 'offshore immigration detention centre' (the others are Nauru and Manus). These centres hold people who have tried to reach Australia, usually by sea, and claim asylum. But they have been told that resettlement in Australia is not an option for them, and they are detained for an indefinite period. There are many tragic stories of those who have been held, isolated, with no hope, some of them being moved around these off-shore and on-shore detention facilities for years.

Predictably the Christmas Island detainees suffer a range of mental-health challenges. Many of them endured torture and appallingly difficult events in their own countries, and very tough journeys as they fled. And now they are detained with no freedom to exercise any control over their own lives. A therapist called Poh Lin Lee was employed to provide mental-health support. She wrote an academic paper about the experience, and she was also the subject of an award-winning documentary: *Island of the Hungry Ghosts*.

Her experience on Christmas Island illustrates the importance of having someone who can really hear your story. The detainees have no power to change their situation, and nor does Poh Lin. All she can do is spend time with them, sometimes just for one session, as they are often moved unexpectedly. There is nothing she can do for them materially except hear their stories. Poh Lin was trained in a psychological approach known as Narrative Therapy. One major feature of this method is the use of storytelling to empower people. As one writer on narrative therapy explains: 'It really is about celebrating and appreciating each person's unique story and helping them frame it in a way that is more self-affirming and less self-defeating'.[1] In narrative therapy the story is not provided by the listener, but space is made for it, and it is allowed to be complex and unique. It is not judged. One of the basic assumptions is

---

1   L. Phillips, 'Stories of Empowerment', *Counseling Today*, October 2017, pp. 26–33.

that people can become the primary authors of the stories of their own lives and find an identity that reflects their knowledge, inner resources, and skills, so that any problems can be addressed.

Poh Lin Lee's focus is on enabling her clients to tell the thickest, richest stories of themselves that they can – not thin stories of torture, suffering, and despair, although they are undoubtedly true. She supports them to find more – to find their resilience, the acts of resistance, their values, their very identity. She enables Mohammed to find his memories of the countryside of his childhood. She meets Daryoush, who describes himself as a 'bad man'. To help him reconnect with an identity that is capable and caring, she invites him to tell her the story of his life as a dynamic community-minded entrepreneur before he left Iran. When Ali describes how everyone in his life disappears, he and Poh Lin agree to say goodbye at the end of every session, just in case it proves to be the last. This is the principle of '*Making now precious*', which is also the title of her account of her work in the detention centre.

We are of course not acting as therapists in our own encounters, nor would we want to be. But we can learn from narrative therapy the importance of hearing the stories of others without judgement and, if we can, helping our friends to tell more of their stories, to help them realise how strong and unique they are.

Lee's affirmation of 'Making now precious' leads me back to the work of Martin Buber. It is such a beautiful intention to have in our interactions. He writes: 'A human being becomes whole not in virtue of a relation to himself (only) but rather in virtue of an authentic relation to another human being.'[2] Sharing the stories of our real experiences puts us in an authentic relation with another human being. And therefore it is in that relationship that there is the possibility for us to move towards wholeness.

---

2   M. Buber, *I and Thou*, translated by Ronald Gregor Smith (New York: Charles Scribner's Sons, 1958).

I end with some words by the Uruguayan writer, Eduardo Galeano: 'Scientists say that human beings are made of atoms, but a little bird told me that we are also made of stories.'[3]

Question for Reflection and Discussion

What is your experience of sitting with others' stories of suffering? To what extent do you feel we have an obligation to listen to such stories and bear witness to tough realities?

---

3   Eduardo Galeano, *Democracy Now!* (8 May 2013).

9 Me or We?

I would like to start with some words by Buddhadasa Bhikku:

> The entire cosmos is a cooperative. The sun, the moon, and the stars live together as a cooperative. When we realize that the world is a mutual, interdependent, cooperative enterprise, that human beings are all mutual friends in the process of birth, old age, suffering and death, then we build a noble, even heavenly environment. If our lives are not based in this truth, then we shall perish.[1]

Yesterday I talked about our own stories, how they form our identity as individuals with unique experiences, and the benefits of telling them and being heard. Today I will broaden the theme, as our individual stories show how we are entwined with what is going on in the wider world, if we can recognise that. Accepting that this is the case opens our eyes to injustices that we might not have been aware of.

We are all parts of multiple systems: the ecological systems that make up the whole of life on planet Earth; but also economic systems, organisations, and society. Recognising that we exist in a wider world of systems that affect us means that we can recognise that any difficulties that confront us are probably not due to personal failings but to a system that restricts certain groups, or an environment that fails to provide opportunities, or a society that tells us that some people have less value than others.

Now may I introduce you to W. E. B. Du Bois (1868–1963), who was an African American sociologist, historian, civil-rights activist, Pan-Africanist, author, poet, researcher, and editor (and the first African American to be awarded a PhD at Harvard). Taiwo Afuape and Gillian Hughes explain that Du Bois, and later the French philosopher Michel Foucault,

---

1   http://fore.research.yale.edu/religion/buddhism/index.html

understood dominant knowledges as stories or discourses (the spoken, written or behavioural expectations shared within a social or cultural group) that are dominant because they are accepted as 'truth', not questioned, and are maintained by social structures. 'Subjugated' knowledges, stories or discourses are those which are ignored or dismissed; such as the experiences, views or values of those who are marginalised. Du Bois argued that we are ever-confined by our social, cultural and historical position in the world but potentially emancipated by our appreciation of the ways we are oppressed.[2]

So what Foucault is saying is that the dominant stories are the ones with the power, the ones that have been internalised by the individual concerned. They are the lens through which individuals interpret the events of their lives and shape their own identity. This means that not only do we sometimes tell or believe a single story; these narratives are also often the stories of those in power – thin stories that oppress us.

When I discovered Liberation Psychology, it blew my mind. It is the complete opposite of a culture that tells us that if we meditate more, if we remember to write our gratitude diaries, if we volunteer for good causes, if we exercise enough, we will be able to fix our anxiety or our depression. Liberation psychology is the opposite of the ideology that tells us that we are poor because we are not thrifty enough, or not organised enough.

From a Liberation Psychology perspective, we try to understand the person within their context – sociopolitical, cultural, and historical. Therefore, we understand that their distress can be understood not only as an individual problem; we see them in the context of an unjust environment that psychologises and individualises their suffering. This realisation turns things on their head, and we recognise that negative elements of the political and economic environment and social structures are the root causes of distress.

---

2   T. Afuape and G. Hughes, *Liberation Psychology: Towards Emotional Wellbeing through Dialogue* (London, Routledge, 2018).

The negative dominant social narratives and oppressions are often internalised. Naming these injustices, along with telling stories of resistance, promotes well-being. A system of oppression – discrimination, exclusion, deprivation, stress, poverty – leads to internalised oppression, with resultant feelings of hopelessness, helplessness, anger, shame, a sense of inferiority, and vulnerability to psychological distress and addiction. People may feel that their struggles are the result of personal failure. This has two consequences: firstly that if the struggles are due to personal failure, they are difficult to fix; and secondly that failure has become part of their identity.

Naming, and thus externalising, the oppression and negative narrative in itself promotes well-being. The story of injustice and acts of strength and resilience can be uncovered and reinforced, and then those who have been oppressed gain a sense of urgency to take action. Removing problems from the realm of personal failure empowers people.

Imagine being a young refugee in the UK. Life is very hard, because the asylum system is grindingly depressing, and education and social care provision are inadequate. You feel hopeless. Furthermore, the dominant social discourse is of refugees arriving like a swarm, an invasion, a drain on the economy, and this story permeates your identity. You come to feel that you are a 'rubbish person'. But all this can change if you are given support to see your strengths. If you can see that the system is unfair, then this takes away your sense of personal failure. And, if you can recognise that the social discourse is a story that helps politicians, but does not necessarily tell the truth, then this will take the power out of the story and allow space for your own individual, authentic story.

The London-based clinical psychologist and systemic psychotherapist Taiwo Afuape has this to say:

> I became a psychologist/therapist because my heart believed that our stories and how we listen to each other are important. I started to see that collaborative, intimate and responsive conversations do make a difference. They have the potential to generate possibilities where none seemed to exist before.

We are the stories we tell and the stories that are told about us and, ultimately, stories are unfinished. We do people a disservice, and perhaps harm, when we reduce their lives to slogans and treat them as though they do not have complex, rich and moving stories to tell. Working with individuals does not have to mean reverting to individualistic concepts and solutions when we stay open to the social constraints on people's lives and their resistance to these.

I continue to be shaped by these conversations and the people I am privileged to meet: looking out for gems and finding them, becoming more committed to equality, creativity and humanity.[3]

For liberation psychology, the personal is political. Much as we would like to keep politics out of things – perhaps we are worried that getting into politics will lead to conflict, perhaps we feel that the whole political system is broken and even irrelevant – the fact is that politics shapes everything. The Covid crisis really highlighted this, as the decisions of politicians shaped our lives directly and instantly; but austerity, the state of the planet, the stories we tell about oppressed peoples, are all driven by politics. We may feel that our interpersonal relationships, and our church groups, should be outside the political discourse. I understand this wish, but if we don't recognise the influence of politics on people's lives, what are we saying to those around us? That, for example, it's their fault that they can't find somewhere affordable to live, or that their impending homelessness is not something that can be spoken about? Some of us may be somewhat cushioned from the effects of political decisions and societal discourses. If so, we need to recognise how lucky we are; but we cannot live outside these systems and, in order to hear the authentic experiences of those around us, we need to recognise and not dismiss the effects of the political environment on all our lives.

As I was preparing these talks, I became aware of a very large elephant in the room, something that I needed to address. In the relationship between two people – the *I–Thou relation,* as Martin Buber would put

---

3   https://repository.tavistockandportman.ac.uk/1208/1/Afuape

it – we have a vision of one person as the teller and one as the listener. As I use analogies and examples from counselling – which has drawn extensively on Martin Buber's work – and from the world of refugee support, I sometimes get stuck in the thinking that says that there will be a sharer of life stories and a 'sharee'. The danger is that we become stuck in these roles and get drawn into the roles of rescuer and victim, like parts in a play which again provide a limited identity for both parties.

How can these different roles be encapsulated in one whole person? Maybe it's just me, but I feel that it's too easy to get stuck in a role which is only part of our story. As an example, maybe with one specific person we can get trapped in a role where we are often giving advice but then find ourselves unable to ask for help ourselves. Limiting our roles may feel like the safest thing: we stay within our comfort zone, and we interact in ways that feel familiar and predictable. Safe in our role, however, we reduce the authenticity of the encounter.

Walt Whitman, in his grand poem, 'Song of Myself',[4] undergoes an epic journey through a long catalogue of examples of American life. The poem includes the famous lines *Do I contradict myself? Very well, then I contradict myself, I am large, I contain multitudes.* It tells an expansive story, it opens our eyes to the fact that we are not limited by one or two roles: we have an almost infinite capacity. Likewise Thich Nhat Hanh: 'Can we look at each other and recognize ourselves in each other?'. [5]

In the same way, we need to meet our fellow humans where they are, in whatever role works in that moment, open to whatever we find. And so the I–Thou relationship could be expressed as a 'Truly Us' relationship, a genuinely authentic encounter. In this thing that we call life we all have complexities, we all contain multitudes, and we are all connected. Our differences and similarities ebb and flow with life. In the words of Martin Buber that I have already shared with you: 'Actual humanity only exists when we can truly be ourselves and be seen and

---

4   Walt Whitman, 'Song of Myself', in *Leaves of Grass* (1855).
5   Thich Nhat Hanh (blogpost 2020) https://plumvillage.org/articles/please-call-me-by-my-true-names-song-poem

celebrated by the other person'. And as Walt Whitman expressed it in 'Song of Myself': 'I am the mate and companion of people, all just as immortal and fathomless as myself'.

The Unitarian Universalist minister Victoria Safford writes joyfully:

> I will not speak about acceptance of 'other' people with some 'other' kind of lifestyle. I can only look in laughing wonder at human life in all its incarnations. I can taste only in passing the breath of the spirit of life on my mouth and understand our common longing to breathe in deep, deep gulps of it. I cannot think of being anybody else's 'ally' even, because even that implies some degree of separation – some degree of safety for some of us, not all. We are 'allied' with no one and with nothing but love – the larger Love transcending all our understanding, within which all the different, differing, gorgeously various, variant, beautifully deviant aspects of ourselves are bound in elegant unity.[6]

Question for Reflection and Discussion

When (if ever) have you experienced being in something like a genuine I–Thou relationship? How did it feel? What might prevent us from forming genuine I–Thou connections with other people?

---

6   Any Other Questions? | WorshipWeb | UUA.org

10 What We Can't See – Invisible, Misunderstood, Marginalised, and Vilified

In our exploration of telling the truth of our lived experiences, I want to look further at those lives and experiences that are invisible, that are not told, that are not heard. And also those who are not heard because the stereotypes, the dominant discourses, are so loud that they deafen us to the reality of the individuality and complexity of the truth, the true experiences of people who are sometimes portrayed as one-dimensional clichés.

Is anyone here a fan of *Queer Eye*? It's an American reality-TV show released on Netflix that connects people in need of 'more than a makeover', really a life re-boot, with a group of four queer men and one non-binary queen, known as the Fab Five. Episodes are often very touching, with participants supported to engage in difficult conversations with family members or friends, to feel better about themselves, to be able to look to the future and make much-needed changes in their lives. I love it! And my daughter Lizzie is also a fan, and we always talk about the episodes together. She cries even more than I do.

One participant – Steph from New Orleans – was living with her partner Rachel but, following a horrible homophobic incident and a continuous stream of negativity, she felt ashamed of who she was and covered that up with a uniform of sports-supporter gear, to 'make other people more comfortable'. The narrative that was being told about her was that she had to hide. And she believed it and hid behind being a sports superfan. This story may be familiar to some of you. If it is, I am so sorry. It certainly touched our friend Lizzie, who has been shouted at in the street for dressing in her signature colourful rainbow style.

It was not only the abusive incident that created an internalised homophobia which had become normal for Steph, but a constant stream of hostile looks and comments, and the societal discourse which assumes that lesbians live in the big north-eastern cities and California, and not in the South and definitely not in New Orleans. Her limited lifestyle had also become normal. She had made herself invisible.[1]

* * * * * *

If we're talking about invisibility, of *course* the Australian government very deliberately detains asylum seekers offshore indefinitely, as with those living in limbo on Christmas Island. But there are many others who are equally invisible, ignored, misunderstood, marginalised, vilified. And many of these are much, much, much closer to home than Christmas Island! Today I challenge you to think of those in your community, in your location, in your interest group who are invisible right now. And, of course, keen listeners among you will have spotted what I have missed out: what about those who would be in your interest group, your workplace, your church, but are excluded? I want to challenge you by saying that it can be easier for us to care about those detained on Christmas Island, and criticise the Australian government for keeping them there, than to look at our own communities and acknowledge those who are invisible, and our own part in excluding them. Let's spend a few quiet moments, thinking of who might be invisible to us.

* * * * * *

In some ways, the Covid pandemic exposed some of this invisible multitude: elderly people, people living with disabilities in care homes, the elderly living alone or being cared for at home, people with mental-health difficulties. We also realised that there is an invisible army of low-paid workers who are essential in getting us the food we need and keeping the country running.

As a foster carer, I am becoming aware of another invisible group: those who have suffered from childhood trauma, or adverse childhood experiences (sometimes known as ACEs). When I had a spare bedroom,

---

1   *Queer Eye*, Series 7, episode 2.

I was regularly being sent information about young people who needed a placement. Just reading the profiles was enormously saddening: young people with adoption breakdowns, young people whose parents had been sent to prison for long periods for abusing them, young people who had suffered multiple moves, or neglect. These are the young people who eat dry instant noodles to remember when they were six years old and no-one fed them and their younger siblings. These are the young people who drink alcohol and get into fights because they don't know another way of dealing with difficult feelings. As these young people develop into adults, their childhood experiences will still be affecting them physically and mentally, but the young people will be completely invisible. Indeed, most people with mental-health problems are invisible, as well as those with so-called invisible physical disabilities and chronic health issues. Drug addiction, gambling, alcoholism, and domestic violence are also invisible, and often hidden in shame.

Poverty can also be invisible, and those of us who are comfortably off should not fall into the trap of thinking that someone 'like us' can't be struggling financially. Homelessness, especially sofa surfing, is another situation that may well be hidden from us.

So what can we do to ensure that we see those who are invisible? We need to be open, aware, read those stories of invisible lives, watch those TV shows, not so that we can know about the lives of everyone who is invisible – that would be impossible, because everyone is unique – not so that we can understand all the oppressions that have led to that point: we should never be telling someone what their story is! We need to read or watch different stories to open our minds to how the world is for some people, and challenge some of our own preconceptions.

In Canada, at the launch of public events there is sometimes an acknowledgement of the original owners of the land on which the event is taking place. The Land Acknowledgment for Ottawa is: 'We [I] would like to begin by acknowledging that the land on which we gather is the traditional unceded territory of the Algonquin Anishnaabeg people.' This practice renders visible the often invisible indigenous First Nation population, prompting recognition of an existence which was denied by the colonisers' appropriation of land, forced assimilation, and erasure of memories.

As well as our LGBT siblings such as Steph in New Orleans, about whom I spoke earlier, our trans siblings are having a difficult time right now, with campaigns that claim to be trying to protect children but are actually stirring up fear and hatred for trans women and men. The result is that trans teens suffer worse mental health and victimisation. That is not protecting children. Daniel Radcliffe cut to the heart of it when he said that adults need to 'trust kids to tell them who they are'. I think he's on to something there. We can continue in a similar vein:

- Trust people of colour to tell you what's happening. Don't deny their experiences of racism and oppression.
- Trust people with invisible disabilities to tell you what life is like for them. Don't google their disorder and then ask if they've tried this or that 'remedy'.
- Trust those in poverty when they tell you how hard life is. Don't give them recipes for porridge and lentil soup.
- Trust people who have suffered trauma to tell you how it has affected their lives. Don't offer up solutions as if they haven't already tried to help themselves.
- Trust people who are neurodiverse to tell you what is difficult and what is helpful. Don't act as though they're just not trying hard enough, or make the exact same adjustment that you do for your autistic nephew.

Both Jesus and the Prophet Mohammed made a point of including those who were traditionally excluded. We all know the tale of the Good Samaritan: a foreigner who cares for a member of a different group and is seen to be truly a good neighbour. Jesus constantly looked around him as he travelled about and truly *saw* many people who were invisible to others: tax collectors, lepers, blind people, sick people, poor widows, children, sinful women, foreigners. Through my youngest son I have learned a lot about Islam, a faith which is also built on a base of equality, with Bilal Ibn Rabah, a freed slave from Ethiopia, said to be the first Muezzin – the one who sings the public call to prayer.

Whether visible or invisible, those who are different from the standard white male archetype are often stereotyped with thin, often prejudicial narratives. The residents of Grenfell Tower, ironically a high-rise building which was and is far from invisible, were treated as *less than*, as unimportant. A carelessness or thoughtlessness was at work, a concern for appearances rather than valuing the safety of those living there. Many of the residents were people of colour, low paid, migrants, refugees. More importantly, they were perceived as 'different'.

* * * * * *

So we try to notice and interrogate the dominant narrative. This is the reason why certain groups are marginalised, why they are vilified. This narrative is thin, it puts people into boxes, it limits them, and it stops our minds being open to the authentic stories of each person as an individual and not a stereotype. The dominant narrative overshadows individual stories and makes the individual invisible, hidden underneath.

The dominant narrative that says we need always to be positive – 'look on the bright side' – is another reason why people can make themselves invisible. When there is pressure to be positive, to be OK, to see the silver lining in every cloud, we may, either consciously or unconsciously, keep our authentic experiences hidden. When things are going badly, a cursory 'How are you?' doesn't feel like the moment for anything more than a 'Fine, thanks'.

Sometimes the dominant narrative is not that we or our stories are unacceptable in some way, but that they are trivial, banal, or boring – just not worth telling. When my first child was about six months old, I booked myself on a philosophy study day in London (I live in Surrey). It was the first time I had been away from her for a substantial period of time, and while I was sitting in the Tube I was desperate to tell all the strangers around me 'I have a baby, you know! She's not with me right now, but I have a baby.' At the seminar we started to explore the work of Luce Irigaray (a French feminist, philosopher, and psychoanalyst). To be honest I can't really remember much about it, but I recall the tutor saying something like 'Irigaray wanted to bring the stories of women into the narrative: domestic chores and household tasks are worth writing about'. And a young man interrupted and said 'But that's just boring isn't it?'. That, of course, proved the tutor's point and showed exactly how some stories are dismissed. On a personal level it also diminished my life and devalued me, as a stay-at-home mum with a baby.

All stories, from all people, are important. If a story is being told about a certain group, take a minute to question that story, and look beneath or beyond it for the authentic stories of each individual. To quote the American writer Rebecca Solnit: 'A free person tells her own story', and 'A valued person lives in a society in which her story has a place'.[2] May we be able to listen to all the stories, and may we work towards making a society in which every story is valued.

Question for Reflection and Discussion

How open are you to seeking alternative perspectives that counter the 'dominant narrative' that is shaped by the powerful? Where might you go to seek out voices that tell a different story?

---

2   R. Solnit, 'Silence and powerlessness go hand in hand – women's voices must be heard', Guardian, 8 March 2017, https://www.theguardian.com/commentisfree/2017/mar/08/silence-powerlessness-womens-voices-rebecca-solnit.

11 Making Space

I have introduced some ideas about our stories, how they shape our identity, and how we can try to look beyond the thin stories to the thick, rich stories of our lives. I have touched on the invisibility of certain groups, the misunderstood, the victimised and vilified, and stressed how important it is to be open to hearing all stories without prejudice.

I have referred to the thinking of Martin Buber. One of his great legacies was the recognition of the central importance of truly authentic relationships between people. He writes: 'When two people relate to each other authentically and humanly, God is the electricity that surges between them.'[1] So in our genuine, open interactions with each other, we are truly creating the divine. Whatever your belief about the nature of the divine, this is powerful stuff. When we tell the truth of our lived experiences to someone who is really listening, this is what Buber would call an 'I–Thou' encounter. An I–Thou relationship is one in which both parties fully recognise and accept each other. For Buber, this relationship is the basis of human wholeness.

Today I want to talk about the sacred, human, life-affirming work of ensuring that there are places and times when we can all be our authentic selves and share the truth of our lived experience. It seems to me that we need three things: the physical (or online) space, the time, and the intention to provide a safe space for sharing the truth of our lives. We need to feel safe, to feel that those we are sharing with will listen and not judge, will be open to our reality and not dismiss it. So we need to know those people with whom we share our life experiences, enough that we trust them with that which is precious and authentic. I still have a memory from my youth of a church minister disclosing something that I had told him in confidence. It has stayed with me although it was more than 35 years ago, and I am even now appalled by this breach of trust.

---

1   M. Buber, *I and Thou* (New York: Charles Scribner's Sons, 1958).

If we want people to tell us how they *really* are, and we feel able to hear that, we need to signal to them somehow that we are open to an authentic encounter. When I work with volunteers running activities for asylum seekers, I advise them to try to cultivate a calm, accepting demeanour so that a young person can feel confident to tell them something if they want to without the volunteer over-reacting with exaggerated sympathy or being shocked or upset. You must hear and hold whatever they want to talk to you about. Thinking back to Steph from *Queer Eye*, it occurs to me that a rainbow badge would be one way to give a positive signal to someone who is uncertain about whether they need to be invisible or not. I don't for one moment think that the problems of the world can be fixed by badges. However, if we meet someone new and we would like to make an authentic connection, it is worth thinking about how we can demonstrate that by our appearance and initial conversation.

And time! How often are we rushing around, busy with our own lives, hurrying to get somewhere and focused on what we need to do? In that state we are not available to listen and really *be* with another person. Lack of time and a task-focus rather than an openness to the people we come across are completely understandable; a hectic schedule and preoccupation with my own stuff is probably my default mode of existence. Actually it feels reassuring to me. Being open to encounters with people, either strangers or friends, might lead to something unpredictable, something beautiful and authentic, but unpredictable. But if we can be open to the uncertainty, then we can also reap unexpected blessings.

Alternatively, we can seek out a space that is structured and controlled, so that we can feel confident and safe to share, even though we don't know everyone very well. These spaces may be meetings of Alcoholics Anonymous, or church engagement groups, or support groups either online or in person, or other groups focused, for example, on creative writing or poetry.

Some of those who belong to traditionally invisible groups are doing amazing work to make their lives visible and therefore increase awareness and understanding of others in their situation. Those of us who wish to step out of our own small worlds and learn more about the real-life experiences of those quite different from ourselves have a wonderful opportunity to learn from all the material that is out there. But honestly sharing online in a public or semi-public space means that strangers or acquaintances may give really vile feedback which can rob us of any sense of safety and make us feel diminished.

In fact there are a lot of reasons why we might be carefully sharing only a part of our life experience, or even being a little misleading. The Instagram effect means that we see the lives of others online and think that they are looking fantastic all the time and having amazing experiences, and so we feel the pressure to curate our own online presence as well. I find that my friends just stop posting when they are going through difficult times. It is completely understandable, but it reinforces the impression that everything that happens is positive. Of course there are others who do post 'warts and all' messages, whatever happens. I appreciate it when they do that, because I am reassured that I am not the only one who struggles sometimes.

The negative effects of sharing online – the rose-tinted Instagram effect, the hostile responses to public posts, and an awareness of all the awfulness that happens online – might make us think that the only way that we can have a true I–Thou relationship is in person: that relating online is somehow inferior and potentially dangerous. But we know that everything changed during the pandemic. Companies made working at home possible for a large proportion of their employees during Covid lockdowns. This continues to a certain extent today, with the numbers working from home higher than before the pandemic. It must be enormously frustrating for those who were trying to persuade employers pre-pandemic to accommodate their disabilities or caring responsibilities by allowing home-working.

And of course social meet-ups and church services went online. The online Heart and Soul gatherings created by Jane Blackall provided an opportunity for anyone with internet access to share in a time of connection. Heart and Soul was, and still is, accessible by many more people than in-person meetings in a building can be: by those who live far away, those with disabilities, or mental-health challenges, or caring responsibilities.

We should ask ourselves 'How are the groups or events that we are involved in excluding people who might be interested?' Is the space that we are making really open to all? Is there anything we can do to open it up? Are there any barriers that we can take down? But there is a conflict here. Any one community has only a limited capacity to run engagement groups and worship services. Some people may be unable to join online. And some of us may prefer to meet in person. In a democratic organisation, where do we put our resources? There was a huge amount of creativity applied to solving these logistical issues during the pandemic, and one advantage of online events is that the participants don't need to be local, so, for example, churches can pool resources. But when circumstances allow and the majority prefers in-person meetings, should we exclude those who can't attend? Hybrid meetings (in-person events which are also online) are one solution to this, which many chapels and churches have embraced. Perhaps we should also acknowledge that there is not always a solution that will suit everyone, but if we approach our planning with the intention of making our events accessible, then we can at least get the issues out in the open and make tough decisions if we need to.

On both an organisational level and a personal level it is so easy to exclude people. My youngest son is an Afghan Muslim, and he dislikes being around people drinking alcohol, a fact which excludes him from many opportunities to socialise. Some neurodivergent people find noisy spaces difficult. From my own experience, and to my shame, I had not even noticed the unacceptable noise level in a particular meeting place until it was pointed out to me.

On the other hand, meaningful encounters are often unplanned, serendipitous. Over the past five years I have been shopping at the only *halal* shop in Guildford, and the owner is someone with whom I definitely have I–Thou moments. He has a son the same age as my youngest and, although I don't actually know his name, I have shared parts of my life with him and his employees. During the pandemic they were the people outside my immediate family whom I saw the most. I value that connection, and my life would be poorer if I were to stop seeing them regularly. It is a connection that I could never have predicted in my life.

So an I–Thou connection, a sharing of our truth, can be really brief and in a public space. Maybe you can recall impromptu, spontaneous encounters with strangers that are so precious – in supermarkets or coffee shops, at bus stops, on trains, in multi-storey car parks. I recently met a lovely couple of women on a Sunday morning trying to get into a multi-storey car park in Leeds. As we worked out how to get in and pay for parking, we chatted about what we had done the night before. With real concern for me, a person they had met only a few minutes before, they checked: 'You're not still drunk, are you?'. No, I wasn't.

* * * * * *

Do you remember New Orleans Steph from yesterday? I think it was Karamo who told her: 'Surround yourself with people who make you feel loved and comfortable'. The Fab Five invited her to a gay bar, and they all brought along their partners to hang out. You could see how relaxed and free she felt, just able to be herself. Sometimes we need to be with people like us, people who understand our life experience. When I began fostering, I had the idea that I myself, my family, and our friends would be enough of a community for my first boy, who is Kurdish. However, when I first took him to college and he met other Kurds, he was a changed young man. He became animated, confident, at ease. He had found the community where he could be himself, speak in his own language, and not have to explain himself. From then on he thrived, and I learned a useful lesson: however nice it is to spend time with a variety of people, there are huge benefits to being with your own community (however you define it) if you can.

* * * * * *

So far I have only touched on human interactions, but now I want to make some space for the divine. I know that in this room there are approximately 40 people, each with their own unique experience and concept of God, Goddess, Spirit, the Universe. I invite you to use whichever name helps you to connect with that which is sacred.

No matter what our conception of God, she, he, they, it should be a safe haven for us to be our own true selves, unconditionally accepted. In the presence of the divine we can speak about our true experiences, be our authentic selves, and know that we are loved. Martin Buber said: 'When two people relate to each other authentically and humanly, God is the electricity that surges between them' – but when we are alone, the divine does not desert us! Connecting with the divine in an authentic and vulnerable way is also a space for us to share the truth of our lives with that which is beyond understanding, and being truly ourselves in that space can be a source of peace and healing.

So my wish is that we can all find I–Thou moments in random encounters, planned meetings, and group settings, and that we can share our stories with others, so that we can be authentically *us*. And in all our interactions may we make space for others to be authentically *them*. In addition perhaps we need to make space in solitude or in community to share the truth of our lives in the presence of the divine as well?

Question for Reflection and Discussion

How might you go about making spaces where it is safer to 'be real' and 'tell the truth' in your own community or context?

---

12 Back to Reality

As I wrote these talks, I was struck by how much we need each other, even though sometimes we tell ourselves that we will be fine on our own. My thoughts go to those who are alone – really alone – and to those who feel alone because, for whatever reason, having an I–Thou encounter with the people around them is not possible. My thoughts go to those who feel they have to make their true selves invisible, and to those who are housebound and therefore invisible to the outside world, or too busy with a night-time cleaning job or caring responsibilities to find that time, that space, to speak and be heard.

As we may have discovered this week, it is not always easy to be in an I–Thou relationship or in a space where we can share the truth of our lived experience. If we find that here, at Summer School, how much more difficult must it be in the real world? Obviously, not having a soundproof study and maid service, I was writing these talks while living in the real world. I have therefore observed over the space of a few days my own I–Thou encounters – planned, serendipitous, individual, or collective. And also the mode of communication that they have used. Here are some examples from the week when I was writing the talks.

1. **Serendipitous.** Preoccupied about an issue with one of my foster kids, I shared it with the owner of the *halal* shop, who I now see is a real mensch. He must engage in dozens of conversations every day, and yet he really listened to what I said and responded in a super-supportive and appropriate way.
2. **Planned.** I met up with a friend and former work colleague and shared (possibly over-shared) issues that were on my mind. As a person with a lot of life experience and also fostering experience and knowledge of the young person herself, having her hear and empathise was so helpful.
3. **Unexpected.** Via WhatsApp I got in touch with a friend, to check how her PhD viva had gone, and hopefully to congratulate her. Sadly it had not gone well, and she was feeling destroyed by the

verdict of the examiners, which hit her totally out of the blue: her supervisors had not raised any issues with her work. So she shared how she was feeling, and the exchange was real and heartfelt.

4. **Summer School panel meeting.** All meetings start with a check-in, just like an engagement group. It's a really nice moment to spend time together just sharing what's going on with us and reminding each other that we are human beings, not machines processing to-do lists!

I consider myself to be extremely lucky and privileged to have all these wonderful connections. It is interesting for me to notice that of these four examples, only two were face to face, and one happened solely via text and emojis. Perhaps you would like to take a minute or two to think about the connections or I–Thou moments that you have had, both here at Summer School and at home.

* * * * * *

Earlier this week we heard part of Ben Okri's heart-breaking poem, 'Grenfell, June 2017'. You can read the whole text at *Grenfell Tower 2017 – A Poem by Ben Okri – Ben Okri Official* Site. I find it almost unbearably moving – but its description of the coming together of community to grieve for the dead, and to support each other, is, for me, another glimpse of the divine. All the best instincts and qualities of humankind were contained in this coming together, this enormous hug in action. Sharing stories is part of the healing, part of the cementing of community which is our strength, because our nature is not to exist completely alone. We need each other. If we can share the story of our true experiences with someone, we are seen, we are known, we are able to touch the divine.

And the proponents of the Liberation Psychology that I spoke about earlier this week have found that sharing stories, then strengthening communities who go on to take action to improve their lives, not only brings people together and makes social change, but it improves the well-being of individuals. As we find our community, and name that which is oppressing us, we feel empowered to work with other people to effect change. We change the story of our own lives, from a despairing one to one where we are a valued member of the community and we regain some control: we feel capable again. From social-housing residents in Ireland to HIV-positive women in London and imprisoned young people, projects inspired by the principles of Liberation Psychology have enabled people to change their lives. There are many inspiring examples, not necessarily explicitly linked to Liberation Psychology – so we know from our own experience that this process works.

And we are all, I am sure, contributing to our own little communities – friend groups, congregations, walking groups, pottery classes (in my case). But the question that we should always be asking is 'Are we including everyone? Who is not here, and why?'. Like me, many of you will have excitedly returned to in-person activities after the Covid lockdown, but has this meant that those people who could only join in online are now excluded?

Conversely, as everyday transactions have moved online or been automated, those opportunities for connection that went alongside the transactions have disappeared. If you work online, you will probably be missing the social aspects of the actual workplace. I used to work in a university office, and the job was fine, but what was great was being with the team, seeing my fellow workers every day. Those interactions and friendships were very precious to me. Even longer ago, when no-one had a mobile phone, and rented houses often had phones that only took incoming calls, I made friends with a woman waiting to use the payphone. Now I, like many people, I suspect, use my mobile as a shield and a comforter. Looking at it rather than looking outwards makes me feel safe, and again I am protected from the unpredictability of interacting with strangers. As Iona Lawrence, formerly of the Jo Cox Foundation, observes:

Humans are social beings, so loneliness is a challenge as old as humanity itself. But globalisation, gentrification, digitisation and automation are playing havoc on the way we connect at home, at work and during leisure time. We share fewer family meals; increasingly connect online instead of face-to-face; increasingly work outside of traditional team environments; increasingly shop online; are less faithful and religious; and are less likely to belong to a trade (or any other kind of) union.[1]

As those natural opportunities for connection and interaction are reducing, the challenge is to create new opportunities, diverse opportunities that are intentional and inclusive. Some can connect only online, some cannot do so at all; some thrive in noisy, busy places, some need peace and quiet.

There are so many beautiful examples of people connecting and reaching out: the fans of the singer Tori Amos who, over many years, have created a loving, supportive community ... the gym in Manchester which values and nurtures older members and those with disabilities, those who struggle to fit into regular gyms ... and the online Twitch community which has evolved from a laddish young-white-male-only environment to a friendly and welcoming space for LGBTQ+, disabled, and neurodivergent gamers.

* * * * * *

For some, sharing even a tiny piece of their true experiences from the past is just too painful, so a focus on speaking about anything that is going on right now (provided that the traumatic events are not ongoing) is a lovely way to share time together. A foster carer whom I know had a child who had been through unimaginable trauma, about which it was impossible to speak. The child and her therapist related wholly in the world of Harry Potter.

Speaking about likes and dislikes, food, films, books, art are also a form of authentic sharing. In our creativity we put ourselves out there. We may choose to express ourselves through a song, or perhaps in fabric

---

1   I. Lawrence, 'My Friend Glenn — Finding Connection in a Disconnected Age', https://ionaflawrence.medium.com/my-friend-glenn-finding-connection-in-a-disconnected-age-31258f858d26 (2018).

work, as Tracy Emin did. Music, pottery, and all creative arts are a way to share who we are. The arts connect us back to ourselves as we try to find our authentic voice.

Activities that are not specifically intended for sharing can be amazing opportunities to have important conversations. Sharing the experience of working or walking alongside someone often opens the possibility for a kind of relaxed openness. Parents of teenagers know this. I know parents who have the best conversations with their kids over the washing up, and I personally have found that table tennis can lead to much more revealing conversations about what's going on at school than just asking 'How was school?' and receiving one of the following stock answers: 'rubbish', 'not bad', 'fine', or 'good'. But while we are engaging in table tennis, a conversation can be much more expansive and free-ranging. For older kids, driving practice is also a marvellous opportunity – once you've got past the beginner stage when pretty much all you are talking about is clutch, brakes, gears, and so on.

We can learn from the big events, the big injustices, the campaigning that many of us are involved in, whether in the areas of climate change, racism, housing, refugee welfare, or poverty, to name just a few. I have spoken about the tragedy of Grenfell Tower and the offshore detention of asylum seekers. Nearer to home, perhaps in this room, in our congregations, and certainly in the area where we live are those who are lonely, those who struggle to get out to events for whatever reason. Perhaps we ourselves are feeling that an aspect of our life is invisible to others. From authentic relationships comes true community, which feels like home. As Maya Angelou says, 'The ache for home lives in all of us, the safe place where we can go as we are and not be questioned'.[2] And in community I truly believe that we can change the world. In the words of Audre Lorde: 'Without community there is no liberation'.[3]

....

2   M. Angelou, *All God's Children Need Travelling Shoes* (Random House, 1986).
3   A. Lorde, 'The Master's Tools Will Never Dismantle the Master's House' (1984) in *Sister Outsider: Essays and Speeches* (Berkeley, CA, Crossing Press, 2007).

As we come to the close of Summer School and prepare to return to our own unique worlds,

May we have the strength to tell our authentic stories.
May we have the space in our lives to create a space for others.
May we be the creators of the divine in our relationships.
May we be the creators of inclusive communities.
And may we realise the power we have to change the world.

Because, as Helen Keller once said: 'Alone, we can do so little; together, we can do so much.'

Question for Reflection and Discussion

Do you feel that you can share the truth of your lived experience? If not, why not?

The author

Louise Baumberg has been a member of Godalming Unitarians for nearly 20 years. She has in the past led the children's programme and has also led services mainly for her home congregation. Her first experience of Hucklow Summer School was in 2008, and she first joined the Summer School panel in 2018. Louise became a foster carer for young refugees in 2017 and gained a Master's degree in Refugee Care in 2021, volunteering and working with local refugee-support organisations alongside her other commitments.

Milton Keynes UK
Ingram Content Group UK Ltd.
UKHW020003230224
438319UK00001B/53

9 780853 190998